Can you repeat that?	**Può ripetere?** pwoh ree·<u>peh</u>·teh·reh
I don't understand.	**Non capisco.** nohn kah·<u>pees</u>·koh
Do you speak English?	**Parla inglese?** <u>pahr</u>·lah een·<u>gleh</u>·zeh
I don't speak Italian.	**Non parlo italiano.** nohn <u>pahr</u>·loh ee·tah·<u>lyah</u>·noh
Where's the restroom [toilet]?	**Dov'è la toilette?** doh·<u>veh</u> lah <u>twah</u>·leht
Help!	**Aiuto!** ah·<u>yoo</u>·toh

Italian
Phrase Book
&
Dictionary

Berlitz Publishing
New York   Munich   Singapore

Contacting the Editors
Every effort has been made to provide accurate information in this publication, but changes are inevitable. The publisher cannot be responsible for any resulting loss, inconvenience or injury. We would appreciate it if readers would call our attention to any errors or outdated information. We also welcome your suggestions; if you come across a relevant expression not in our phrase book, please contact us: Berlitz Publishing, 193 Morris Avenue, Springfield, NJ 07081, USA. E-mail: comments@berlitzbooks.com

Third Printing: February 2008
Printed in Singapore

Publishing Director: Sheryl Olinsky Borg
Senior Editor/Project Manager: Lorraine Sova
Editor: Francesca Romana Onofri
Translation: Publication Services, Inc., Paola Bortolotti-van Loon
Cover Design: Claudia Petrilli
Interior Design: Derrick Lim, Juergen Bartz
Production Manager: Elizabeth Gaynor
Cover Photo: © Royalty-Free/Corbis
Interior Photos: p. 12 ©Studio Fourteen/BrandX/Age Fotostock; p. 16, 160 ©Fabio Loon; p. 17 ©European Central Bank; p. 28 ©Omer Simkha; p. 34 ©Roman Krochuck, 2006/Shutterstock, Inc.; p. 38 ©JupiterImages Corporation/Creatas/Fotosearch.com; p. 49 ©Ryan McVay/Photodisc/Age Fotostock; p. 54, 56 ©Heinz Hebeisen/Iberimage. com; p. 83 ©Ken Welsh/Pixtal/Age Fotostock; p. 75, 87, 90, 120, 133, 146, 158 ©Javier Larrea/Pixtal/Age Fotostock; p. 104 ©Pixtal/Age Fotostock; p. 107 ©2003 IMS Communications Ltd/www.picture-gallery.com/Flat Earth; p. 113 ©Digital Vision; p. 116 ©Iconotec/Alamy; p. 123 ©Digital Vision; p. 140 ©TongRo Image Stock/Alamy; p. 148 ©Royalty-Free/Corbis; p. 150 ©Ingram Publishing/Alamy; p. 153 ©PhotoBliss/Alamy; p. 157 ©David McKee, 2006/Shutterstock, Inc.; p. 168 ©Graham Andrew Reid, 2006/Shutterstock, Inc.; p. 179 ©Nigel Reed/Alamy; Map © H.W.A.C.

Contents

Survival

Food

People

Fun

Special Needs

Resources

Dictionary

Pronunciation

This section is designed to make you familiar with the sounds of Italian using our simplified phonetic transcription. You'll find the pronunciation of the Italian letters and sounds explained below, together with their "imitated" equivalents. This system is used throughout the phrase book; simply read the pronunciation as if it were English, noting any special rules below.

Stress has been indicated in the phonetic pronunciations by underlining. These letters should be pronounced with more emphasis. Generally, the vowel of the next to last syllable is stressed. When a final vowel is stressed, it has an accent.

Consonants

Letter(s)	Approximate Pronunciation	Symbol	Example	Pronunciation
c	1. before e and i, ch as in chip	ch	**cerco**	<u>chehr</u>·koh
	2. elsewhere, c as in cat	k	**conto**	<u>kohn</u>·toh
ch	c as in cat	k	**che**	keh
g	1. before e and i, like j in jet	j	**valigia**	vah·<u>lee</u>·jyah
	2. elsewhere, g as in go	g	**grande**	<u>grahn</u>·deh
gg	pronounced more intensely	dj	**viaggio**	<u>vyah</u>·djoh
gh	g as in go	gh	**ghiaccio**	<u>ghyah</u>·chyoh
gli	lli as in million	lly	**bagaglio**	bah·<u>gah</u>·llyoh
gn	like the first n in onion	ny	**bagno**	<u>bah</u>·nyoh

Letter(s)	Approximate Pronunciation	Symbol	Example	Pronunciation
h	always silent		**ha**	ah
r	rolled in the back of the mouth	r	**Roma**	roh·mah
s	1. generally s as in sit	s	**salsa**	sahl·sah
	2. sometimes z as in zoo	z	**casa**	kah·zah
sc	1. before e and i, sh as in shut	sh	**uscita**	oo·shee·tah
	2. elsewhere, sk as in skin	sk	**scarpa**	skahr·pah
z/zz	1. generally ts as in hits	ts	**grazie**	grah·tsyeh
	2. sometimes a little softer, like dz	dz	**zero**	dzeh·roh

The letters b, d, f, k, l, m, n, p, q, t and v are pronounced as in English. The letters j, k, w, x and y are not true members of the Italian alphabet and appear only in foreign words or names.

Vowels

Letter	Approximate Pronunciation	Symbol	Example	Pronunciation
a	short, as in father	ah	**gatto**	gaht·toh
e	1. like e as in get	eh	**destra**	deh·strah
	2. before a single consonant, sometimes like e in they	ay	**sete**	say·teh

Letter	Approximate Pronunciation	Symbol	Example	Pronunciation
i	ee as in meet	ee	**vini**	<u>vee</u>·nee
o	o as in so	oh	**sole**	<u>soh</u>·leh
u	oo as in boot	oo	**fumo**	<u>foo</u>·moh

Vowel Combinations

Letter	Symbol	Example	Pronunciation
ae	ah·<u>eh</u>	**paese**	pah·<u>eh</u>·zeh
ao	<u>ah</u>·oh	**Paolo**	<u>pah</u>·oh·loh
au	ow	**auto**	<u>ow</u>·toh
eo	<u>eh</u>·oh	**museo**	moo-<u>zeh</u>-oh
eu	<u>eh</u>·oo	**euro**	<u>eh</u>·oo·roh
ei	ay	**lei**	lay
ia	yah	**piazza**	<u>pyah</u>·tsah
ie	yeh	**piede**	<u>pyeh</u>·deh
io	yoh	**piove**	<u>pyoh</u>·veh
iu	yoo	**più**	pyoo
ua	wah	**quale**	<u>kwah</u>·leh
ue	weh	**questo**	<u>kweh</u>·stoh
ui	wee	**qui**	kwee
uo	woh	**può**	pwoh

There are approximately sixty million Italian speakers. Many different dialects add variety and color to the country's linguistic landscape. In addition, Italian is spoken in the southern area of Switzerland.

How to Use This Book

These essential phrases can also be heard on the audio CD.

Sometimes you see two alternatives in italics, separated by a slash. Choose the one that's right for your situation.

Essential

I'm on *vacation [holiday]/business*.	**Sono in *vacanza/viaggio d'affari*.** soh·noh een *vah·kahn·tsah/vyah·djoh dahf·fah·ree*
I'm going to…	**Vado a …** vah·doh ah …
I'm staying at the…Hotel.	**Sono all'hotel …** soh·noh ahl·loh·tehl …

You May See...

DOGANA	customs
MERCE DUTY-FREE	duty-free goods
MERCE DA DICHIARARE	goods to declare

Ticketing

When's the…to Milan?	**A che ora è *il/l'*…per Milano?** ah keh oh·rah eh *eel/l*…pehr mee·lah·noh
– (first) bus	**– (primo) autobus** (pree·moh) ow·toh·boos
– (next) flight	**– (prossimo) volo** (prohs·see·moh) voh·loh
– (last) train	**– (ultimo) treno** (ool·tee·moh) treh·noh

Words you may see written are shown in *You May See* boxes.

Any of the words or phrases preceded by dashes can be plugged into the sentence above.

Italian phrases appear in red.

Read the simplified pronunciation as if it were English. For more on pronunciation, see page 7.

Relationships

Who are you with? **Con chi è?** kohn kee ee

I'm here alone. **Sono da solo♂/sola♀.** <u>soh</u>•noh dah <u>soh</u>•loh♂/<u>soh</u>•lah♀

When's your birthday? **Quando è il suo co**[...] eh eel <u>soo</u>•oh kohm•pl[...]

How old are you? **Quanti anni ha?** kw[...]

I'm...years old. **Ho...anni.** oh...<u>ahn</u>•[...]

When different gender forms apply, the masculine form is followed by ♂; feminine by ♀.

▶For Italian pronouns, see page 172.

Information boxes contain relevant country, culture and language tips.

The arrow indicates a cross reference where you'll find related phrases.

A handshake is a common gesture among strangers or in formal settings. Traditionally, it is expected that a woman be the first to offer her hand. A kiss on both cheeks is used among friends and relatives. A nod and a smile suffice when greeting members of a group of people.

You May Hear...

Parlo poco inglese. <u>pahr</u>•loh <u>poh</u>•koh een•<u>gleh</u>•zeh

Non parlo inglese. nohn <u>pahr</u>•loh een•gleh•zeh

I only speak a little English.

I don't speak English

Expressions you may hear are shown in *You May Hear* boxes.

Color-coded side bars identify each section of the book.

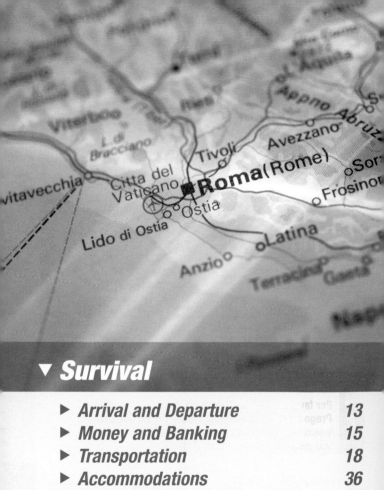

▼ Survival

Arrival and Departure

Essential

I'm on *vacation [holiday]/business.*	**Sono in *vacanza/viaggio d'affari.*** soh·noh een *vah·kahn·tsah/vyah·djoh dahf·fah·ree*
I'm going to…	**Vado a…** vah·doh ah…
I'm staying at the…Hotel.	**Sono all'hotel…** soh·noh ahl·loh·tehl…

You May Hear…

Il passaporto, per favore. eel pahs·sah·pohr·toh pehr fah·voh·reh	Your passport, please.
Motivo della visita? moh·tee·voh dehl·lah vee·zee·tah	What's the purpose of your visit?
Dove alloggia? doh·veh ahl·loh·djah	Where are you staying?
Quanto tempo si ferma? kwahn·toh tehm·poh see fehr·mah	How long are you staying?
Chi viaggia con Lei? kee vyah·djah kohn lay	Who are you traveling with?

Per favore is the standard Italian translation for "please."
Prego is the standard Italian translation for "you are welcome," but it's also used for "please," in the sense of "if you please," in certain informal situations.

Passport Control and Customs

I'm just passing through.

Sono solo di passaggio. <u>soh</u>·noh <u>soh</u>·loh dee pahs·<u>sah</u>·djoh

I'd like to declare…

Vorrei dichiarare… vohr·<u>ray</u> dee·kyah·<u>rah</u>·reh…

I have nothing to declare.

Non ho nulla da dichiarare. nohn oh <u>nool</u>·lah dah dee·kyah·<u>rah</u>·reh

You May Hear…

Ha qualcosa da dichiarare? ah kwahl·<u>koh</u>·zah dah dee·kyah·<u>rah</u>·reh

Anything to declare?

Deve pagare la tassa su questo. <u>deh</u>·veh pah·<u>gah</u>·reh lah <u>tahs</u>·sah soo <u>kweh</u>·stoh

You must pay duty on this.

Apra questa borsa. <u>ah</u>·prah <u>kweh</u>·stah <u>bohr</u>·sah

Open this bag.

You May See…

DOGANA	customs
MERCE DUTY-FREE	duty-free goods
MERCE DA DICHIARARE	goods to declare
NULLA DA DICHIARARE	nothing to declare
CONTROLLO PASSAPORTI	passport control
POLIZIA	police

Money and Banking

Essential

Where's…?	**Dov'è…?** doh·<u>veh</u>…
– the ATM	**– il bancomat** eel <u>bahn</u>·koh·maht
– the bank	**– la banca** lah <u>bahn</u>·kah
– the currency exchange office	**– l'ufficio di cambio** loof·<u>fee</u>·chyoh dee <u>kahm</u>·byoh
When does the bank *open/close*?	**A che ora *apre/chiude* la banca?** ah keh <u>oh</u>·rah <u>ah</u>·preh/<u>kyoo</u>·deh lah <u>bahn</u>·kah
I'd like to change *dollars/pounds* into euros.	**Vorrei cambiare *dei dollari/delle sterline* in euro.** vohr·<u>ray</u> kahm·<u>byah</u>·reh *day <u>dohl</u>·lah·ree/<u>dehl</u>·leh stehr·<u>lee</u>·neh* een <u>eh</u>·oo·roh
I'd like to cash traveler's checks [cheques].	**Vorrei riscuotere dei travellers cheques.** vohr·<u>ray</u> ree·skwoh·<u>teh</u>·reh day <u>trah</u>·vehl·lehrs chehks

ATM, Bank and Currency Exchange

I'd like to change money.	**Vorrei cambiare del denaro.** vohr·<u>ray</u> kahm·<u>byah</u>·reh dehl deh·<u>nah</u>·roh
How much is the fee?	**Quant'è la commissione?** kwahn·<u>teh</u> lah kohm·mees·<u>syoh</u>·neh
I lost *my traveler's checks [cheques]/ credit card.*	**Ho perso *i miei travellers cheques/la mia carta di credito.*** oh <u>pehr</u>·soh *ee mee·<u>ay</u> <u>trah</u>·vehl·lehrs chehks/lah <u>mee</u>·ah <u>kahr</u>·tah dee <u>kreh</u>·dee·toh*
My card *was stolen/doesn't work.*	**La mia carta di credito *è stata rubata/non funziona.*** lah <u>mee</u>·ah <u>kahr</u>·tah dee <u>kreh</u>·dee·toh *eh <u>stah</u>·tah roo·<u>bah</u>·tah/nohn foon·<u>tsyoh</u>·nah*

▶ For bank and credit cards, see page 129.

▶ For numbers, see page 177.

i Cash can be obtained from ATMs with Visa™, Eurocard™, American Express® and many other international cards. Instructions are usually available in English. You can change money at travel agencies and hotels, but the rate will not be as good as at a bank or currency exchange office. Remember to bring your passport when you want to change money.

You May See...

INSERIRE LA CARTA	insert card here
ANNULLA	cancel
CANCELLA	clear
CONFERMA	enter
CODICE SEGRETO	PIN
PRELIEVO	withdrawal
DEPOSITO	deposit
DA CONTO CORRENTE	from checking [current account]
DA CONTO DI RISPARMIO	from savings
RICEVUTA	receipt

You May See...

Italian currency is the **euro €**, divided into 100 **centesimi**.
Coins: 1, 2, 5, 10, 20, 50 **cent**.; €1, 2
Notes: €5, 10, 20, 50, 100, 200, 500

Transportation

Essential

How do I get to town?	**Come si arriva in città?** <u>koh</u>·meh see ahr·<u>ree</u>·vah een cheet·<u>tah</u>
Where's…?	**Dov'è…?** doh·<u>veh</u>…
– the airport	**– l'aeroporto** lah·eh·roh·<u>pohr</u>·toh
– the train [railway] station	**– la stazione ferroviaria** lah stah·<u>tsyoh</u>·neh fehr·roh·<u>vyah</u>·ryah
– the bus station	**– la stazione degli autobus** lah stah·<u>tsyoh</u>·neh <u>deh</u>·llyee <u>ow</u>·toh·boos
– the subway [underground] station	**– la stazione della metropolitana** lah stah·<u>tsyoh</u>·neh <u>dehl</u>·lah meh·troh·poh·lee·<u>tah</u>·nah
How far is it?	**Quanto dista?** <u>kwahn</u>·toh <u>dees</u>·tah
Where do I buy a ticket?	**Dove si comprano i biglietti?** <u>doh</u>·veh see <u>kohm</u>·prah·noh ee bee·<u>llyeht</u>·tee
A *one-way/round-trip [return]* ticket to…	**Un biglietto *di andata/di andata e ritorno* per…** oon bee·<u>llyeht</u>·toh *dee ahn·<u>dah</u>·tah/dee ahn·<u>dah</u>·tah eh ree·<u>tohr</u>·noh* pehr…
How much?	**Quant'è?** kwahn·<u>teh</u>
Is there a discount?	**C'è uno sconto?** cheh <u>oon</u>·oh <u>skohn</u>·toh
Which…?	**Quale…?** <u>kwah</u>·leh…
– gate	**– uscita** oo·<u>shee</u>·tah
– line	**– linea** <u>lee</u>·neh·ah
– platform	**– binario** bee·<u>nah</u>·ryoh

Where can I get a taxi?	**Dove posso trovare un taxi?** <u>doh</u>·veh <u>pohs</u>·soh troh·<u>vah</u>·reh oon <u>tah</u>·ksee
Take me to this address.	**Mi porti a questo indirizzo.** mee <u>pohr</u>·tee ah <u>kweh</u>·stoh een·dee·<u>ree</u>·tsoh
Where's the car rental [hire]?	**Dov'è un autonoleggio?** doh·<u>veh</u> oon ow·toh·noh·<u>leh</u>·djoh
Can I have a map?	**Può darmi una cartina?** pwoh <u>dahr</u>·mee <u>oo</u>·nah kahr·<u>tee</u>·nah

Ticketing

When's the…to Milan?	**A che ora è il/l'…per Milano?** ah keh <u>oh</u>·rah eh eel/l…pehr mee·<u>lah</u>·noh
– (first) bus	– **(primo) autobus** (<u>pree</u>·moh) <u>ow</u>·toh·boos
– (next) flight	– **(prossimo) volo** (<u>prohs</u>·see·moh) <u>voh</u>·loh
– (last) train	– **(ultimo) treno** (<u>ool</u>·tee·moh) <u>treh</u>·noh
Where do I buy a ticket?	**Dove si comprano i biglietti?** <u>doh</u>·veh see <u>kohm</u>·prah·noh ee bee·<u>llyeht</u>·tee
One/Two ticket(s), please.	***Un biglietto/Due biglietti**, per favore.* oon bee·<u>llyeht</u>·toh/<u>doo</u>·eh bee·<u>llyeht</u>·tee pehr fah·<u>voh</u>·reh
For *today/tomorrow.*	**Per *oggi/domani.*** pehr <u>oh</u>·djee/doh·<u>mah</u>·nee

▶ For days, see page 180.

▶ For time, see page 179.

A…ticket.	**Un biglietto…** oon bee·<u>llyeht</u>·toh…
– one-way	– **di andata** dee ahn·<u>dah</u>·tah
– round-trip [return]	– **di andata e ritorno** dee ahn·<u>dah</u>·tah eh ree·<u>tohr</u>·noh
– first class	– **di prima classe** dee <u>pree</u>·mah <u>klahs</u>·seh
– second class	– **di seconda classe** dee seh·<u>kohn</u>·dah <u>klahs</u>·seh
– economy class	– **di classe economica** dee <u>klahs</u>·seh eh·koh·<u>noh</u>·mee·kah

How much?	**Quant'è?** <u>kwahn</u>·teh
Is there a…discount?	**C'è un biglietto ridotto per…?** cheh oon bee·<u>llyeht</u>·toh ree·<u>doht</u>·toh pehr…
– child	**– bambini** bahm·<u>bee</u>·nee
– student	**– studenti** stoo·<u>dehn</u>·tee
– senior citizen	**– anziani** ahn·<u>tsyah</u>·nee
– tourist	**– turisti** too·<u>ree</u>·stee
The *express/local bus/train*, please.	**L'autobus/Il treno espresso/locale, per favore.** <u>low</u>·toh·boos/eel <u>treh</u>·noh eh·<u>sprehs</u>·soh/ loh·<u>kah</u>·leh pehr fah·<u>voh</u>·reh
I have an e-ticket.	**Ho un biglietto elettronico.** oh oon bee·<u>llyeht</u>·toh eh·leht·<u>troh</u>·nee·koh
Can I buy a ticket on the *bus/train*?	**Posso comprare il biglietto *sull'autobus/ sul treno*?** <u>pohs</u>·soh kohm·<u>prah</u>·reh eel bee·<u>llyeht</u>·toh *sool·low·toh·boos/sool <u>treh</u>·noh*
I'd like to…my reservation.	**Vorrei…la prenotazione.** vohr·<u>ray</u>…lah preh·noh·tah·<u>tsyoh</u>·neh
– cancel	**– annullare** ahn·nool·<u>lah</u>·reh
– change	**– cambiare** kahm·<u>byah</u>·reh
– confirm	**– confermare** kohn·fehr·<u>mah</u>·reh

Plane

Getting to the Airport

How much is a taxi to the airport?	**Quant'è la tariffa del taxi fino all'aeroporto?** <u>kwahn</u>·teh lah tah·<u>reef</u>·fah dehl <u>tah</u>·ksee <u>fee</u>·noh ahl·lah·eh·roh·<u>pohr</u>·toh
To…Airport, please.	**All'aeroporto di…, per favore.** ahl·lah·eh·roh·<u>pohr</u>·toh dee…pehr fah·<u>voh</u>·reh

My airline is…	**Parto con *la/l'…* ** <u>pahr</u>·toh kohn *lah/l…*
My flight leaves at…	**Il volo è alle…** eel <u>voh</u>·loh eh <u>ahl</u>·leh…
I'm in a rush.	**Ho fretta.** oh <u>freht</u>·tah
Can you take an alternate route?	**Può prendere un'altra strada?** pwoh <u>prehn</u>·deh·reh oo·<u>nahl</u>·trah <u>strah</u>·dah
Can you drive *faster/slower*?	**Può andare più *velocemente/lentamente*?** pwoh ahn·<u>dah</u>·reh pyoo *veh·loh·cheh·<u>mehn</u>·teh/ lehn·tah·<u>mehn</u>·teh*

You May Hear…

Con che compagnia aerea viaggia? kohn keh kohm·pah·<u>nee</u>·ah ah·<u>eh</u>·reh·ah <u>vyah</u>·djah
What airline are you flying?

Nazionale o internazionale? nah·tsyoh·<u>nah</u>·leh oh een·tehr·nah·tsyoh·<u>nah</u>·leh
Domestic or international?

Quale terminal? <u>kwah</u>·leh tehr·mee·<u>nahl</u>
What terminal?

You May See…

ARRIVI	arrivals
PARTENZE	departures
RITIRO BAGAGLI	baggage claim
SICUREZZA	security
VOLI NAZIONALI	domestic flights
VOLI INTERNAZIONALI	international flights
CHECK-IN	check-in
CHECK-IN CON BIGLIETTO ELETTRONICO	e-ticket check-in
USCITA	exit

Check-in and Boarding

Where's check-in?	**Dov'è il check-in?** doh·<u>veh</u> eel <u>chehk</u>·een
My name is…	**Mi chiamo…** mee <u>kyah</u>·moh…
I'm going to…	**Vado a…** <u>vah</u>·doh ah…
How much luggage is allowed?	**Quanti bagagli si possono portare?** <u>kwahn</u>·tee bah·<u>gah</u>·llyee see <u>pohs</u>·soh·noh pohr·<u>tah</u>·reh
Which *terminal/gate*?	**Quale *terminal/uscita*?** <u>kwah</u>·leh *tehr·mee·<u>nahl</u>/oo·<u>shee</u>·tah*
I'd like *a window/ an aisle* seat.	**Vorrei un posto vicino *al finestrino/ al corridoio*.** vohr·<u>ray</u> oon <u>poh</u>·stoh vee·<u>chee</u>·noh *ahl fee·neh·<u>stree</u>·noh/ ahl kohr·ree·<u>doh</u>·yoh*
When do we *leave/arrive*?	**Quando *partiamo/arriviamo*?** <u>kwahn</u>·doh *pahr·<u>tyah</u>·moh/ahr·ree·<u>vyah</u>·moh*
Is the flight delayed?	**Il volo è in ritardo?** eel <u>voh</u>·loh eh een ree·<u>tahr</u>·doh
How late?	**Di quanto è in ritardo?** dee <u>kwahn</u>·toh eh een ree·<u>tahr</u>·doh

You May Hear…

Il prossimo! eel <u>prohs</u>·see·moh	Next!
Il suo *passaporto/biglietto*, per favore. eel <u>soo</u>·oh *pahs·sah·<u>pohr</u>·toh/bee·<u>llyeht</u>·toh* pehr fah·<u>voh</u>·reh	Your *passport/ticket*, please.
Quanti bagagli consegna? <u>kwahn</u>·tee bah·<u>gah</u>·llyee kohn·<u>seh</u>·nyah	How many bags are you checking?
Ha il bagaglio in eccesso. ah eel bah·<u>gah</u>·llyoh een eh·<u>chehs</u>·soh	You have excess luggage.

È troppo grande per portarlo a mano.
eh <u>trohp</u>·poh <u>grahn</u>·deh pehr
pohr·<u>tahr</u>·loh ah <u>mah</u>·noh

That's too large for a carry-on [piece of hand luggage].

Ha fatto Lei le valigie? ah <u>faht</u>·toh
lay leh vah·<u>lee</u>·jyeh

Did you pack these bags yourself?

Qualcuno le ha dato qualcosa da portare? kwahl·<u>koo</u>·noh leh ah <u>dah</u>·toh
kwahl·<u>koh</u>·zah dah pohr·<u>tah</u>·reh

Did anyone give you anything to carry?

Vuoti le tasche. <u>vwoh</u>·tee leh <u>tahs</u>·keh

Empty your pockets.

Tolga le scarpe. <u>tohl</u>·gah leh <u>skahr</u>·peh

Take off your shoes.

Imbarco immediato... eem·<u>bahr</u>·koh
eem·meh·<u>dyah</u>·toh...

Now boarding...

Luggage

Where is/Where are...?	**Dov'è/Dove sono...?** doh·<u>veh</u>/<u>doh</u>·veh <u>soh</u>·noh...
– the luggage carts [trolleys]	**– i carrelli per i bagagli** ee kahr·<u>rehl</u>·lee pehr ee bah·<u>gah</u>·llyee
– the luggage lockers	**– il deposito bagagli** eel deh·<u>poh</u>·see·toh bah·<u>gah</u>·lyee
– the baggage claim	**– il ritiro bagagli** eel ree·<u>tee</u>·roh bah·<u>gah</u>·llyee
My luggage has been *lost/stolen*.	**Mi hanno *perso/rubato* i bagagli.** mee <u>ahn</u>·noh <u>pehr</u>·soh/roo·<u>bah</u>·toh ee bah·<u>gah</u>·llyee
My suitcase has been damaged.	**La mia valigia è danneggiata.** lah <u>mee</u>·ah vah·<u>lee</u>·jyah eh dahn·neh·<u>djah</u>·tah

Finding Your Way

Where is/Where are…?	**Dov'è/Dove sono…?** doh·<u>veh</u>/<u>doh</u>·veh <u>soh</u>·noh…
– the currency exchange	**– il cambio valuta** eel <u>kahm</u>·byoh vah·<u>loo</u>·tah
– the car rental [hire]	**– l'autonoleggio** l·<u>ow</u>·toh·noh·<u>leh</u>·djoh
– the exit	**– l'uscita** loo·<u>shee</u>·tah
– the taxis	**– i taxi** ee <u>tah</u>·ksee
Is there… into town?	**C'è…per andare in città?** cheh…pehr ahn·<u>dah</u>·reh een cheet·<u>tah</u>
– a bus	**– un autobus** oon <u>ow</u>·toh·boos
– a train	**– un treno** oon <u>treh</u>·noh
– a subway [underground]	**– una metropolitana** <u>oo</u>·nah meh·troh·poh·lee·<u>tah</u>·nah

▶For directions, see page 33.

Train

Where's the train [railway] station?	**Dov'è la stazione ferroviaria?** doh·<u>veh</u> lah stah·<u>tsyoh</u>·neh fehr·roh·<u>vyah</u>·ryah
How far is it?	**Quanto dista?** <u>kwahn</u>·toh <u>dees</u>·tah
Where is/Where are…?	**Dov'è/Dove sono…?** doh·<u>veh</u>/<u>doh</u>·veh <u>soh</u>·noh…
– the ticket office	**– la biglietteria** lah bee·llyeht·teh·<u>ree</u>·ah
– the information desk	**– l'ufficio informazioni** loof·<u>fee</u>·chyoh een·fohr·mah·<u>tsyoh</u>·nee
– the luggage lockers	**– il deposito bagagli** eel deh·<u>poh</u>·see·toh bah·<u>gah</u>·llyee
– the platforms	**– i binari** ee bee·<u>nah</u>·ree

▶For directions, see page 33.

▶For ticketing, see page 19.

You May See...

BINARI	platforms
INFORMAZIONI	information
PRENOTAZIONI	reservations
SALA D'ATTESA	waiting room
ARRIVI	arrivals
PARTENZE	departures

Questions

Can I have a schedule [timetable]?	**Mi può dare un orario?** mee pwoh <u>dah</u>·reh oon oh·<u>rah</u>·ryoh
How long is the trip?	**Quanto dura il viaggio?** <u>kwahn</u>·toh <u>doo</u>·rah eel <u>vyah</u>·djoh
Do I have to change trains?	**Devo cambiare?** <u>deh</u>·voh kahm·<u>byah</u>·reh

Rail travel is extremely popular and one of the best ways to see Italy, especially with the faster—and more expensive—trains that link major cities. **Eurostar** and **InterCity** are the fastest trains, while **diretti, regionali** and **interregionali** are local trains—ideal to reach smaller towns. Tickets must be stamped before travel in one of the many machines on station concourses and platforms.

Departures

Which track [platform] to...?	**Da che binario parte il treno per...?** dah keh bee·<u>nah</u>·ryoh <u>pahr</u>·teh eel <u>treh</u>·noh pehr...
Is this the *track [platform]/train* to...?	**È il *binario/treno* per...?** eh eel *bee·<u>nah</u>·ryoh/ <u>treh</u>·noh* pehr...

| Where is track [platform]…? | **Dov'è il binario…?** doh·<u>veh</u> eel bee·<u>nah</u>·ryoh… |
| Where do I change for…? | **Dove devo cambiare per…?** <u>doh</u>·veh <u>deh</u>·voh kahm·<u>byah</u>·reh pehr… |

Italians use the 24-hour clock in schedules and other official documents and situations. In other words, the morning hours from 1:00 a.m. to 12:00 noon are the same as in English; after that, just add 12. So, 1:00 p.m. would be 13:00, 5:00 p.m. would be 17:00 and so on.

▶For time, see page 179.

Boarding

| Can I *sit here/open the window*? | **Posso *sedermi qui/aprire il finestrino*?** <u>pohs</u>·soh *seh·<u>dehr</u>·mee kwee/ah·<u>pree</u>·reh eel fee·neh·<u>stree</u>·noh* |
| That's my seat. | **Questo posto è mio.** <u>kweh</u>·stoh <u>poh</u>·stoh eh <u>mee</u>·oh |

You May Hear…

Biglietti, per favore. bee·<u>llyeht</u>·tee pehr fah·<u>voh</u>·reh	Tickets, please.
Deve cambiare a Parma. <u>deh</u>·veh kahm·<u>byah</u>·reh ah <u>pahr</u>·mah	You have to change at Parma.
Prossima fermata: Pisa. <u>prohs</u>·see·mah fehr·<u>mah</u>·tah <u>pee</u>·zah	Next stop, Pisa.

Bus

Where's the bus station?	**Dov'è la stazione degli autobus?** doh·<u>veh</u> lah stah·<u>tsyoh</u>·neh deh·<u>llyee</u> ow·toh·boos
How far is it?	**Quanto dista?** <u>kwahn</u>·toh <u>dees</u>·tah
How do I get to…?	**Come si arriva a…?** <u>koh</u>·meh see ahr·<u>ree</u>·vah ah…
Is this the bus to…?	**È l'autobus per…?** eh <u>low</u>·toh·boos pehr…
Can you tell me when to get off?	**Può dirmi quando scendere?** pwoh <u>deer</u>·mee <u>kwahn</u>·doh <u>shehn</u>·deh·reh
Do I have to change buses?	**Devo cambiare (autobus)?** <u>deh</u>·voh kahm·<u>byah</u>·reh (<u>ow</u>·toh·boos)
Stop here, please!	**Si fermi qui, per favore!** see <u>fehr</u>·mee kwee pehr fah·<u>voh</u>·reh

▶ For ticketing, see page 19.

i When traveling by bus, purchase your ticket before boarding from a tobacconist or from a vending machine at train or subway stations. Tickets have a magnetic strip on the back. Upon boarding the bus, validate your ticket at one of the yellow validation machines on the bus (see picture on page 28). Insert your ticket into the machine with the arrow toward you and pointing downward. The machine will accept the ticket and then return it; a green light shows the ticket is valid and a red light means it is invalid. If the machine does not work, you can try another machine on the bus or write the date, time of day and the bus number on the ticket. If the bus features only the older orange machines, fold the ticket in half lengthwise so that it fits into the machine for validation.

The Italian public transportation system is extensive and generally efficient. Urban areas are served by networks of buses, trams and subways. Tickets are usually sold at **edicole** (newsstands), nearby **caffè** (coffee bars) and **tabacchi** (tobacconists). Discounts are available but vary between locations. Ask the hotel concierge or your travel agent for a schedule.

You May See...

FERMATA AUTOBUS	bus stop
ENTRATA/USCITA	enter/exit
CONVALIDA BIGLIETTO	stamp your ticket

Subway [Underground]

Where's the subway [underground] station?	**Dov'è la stazione della metropolitana?** doh-<u>veh</u> lah stah-<u>tsyoh</u>-neh <u>dehl</u>-lah meh-troh-poh-lee-<u>tah</u>-nah
A map, please.	**Una cartina, per favore.** <u>oo</u>-nah kahr-<u>tee</u>-nah pehr fah-<u>voh</u>-reh
Which line for…?	**Che linea devo prendere per…?** keh <u>lee</u>-neh-ah <u>deh</u>-voh <u>prehn</u>-deh-reh pehr…
Do I have to transfer [change]?	**Devo cambiare?** <u>deh</u>-voh kahm-<u>byah</u>-reh
Is this the subway [train] to…?	**È la metropolitana per…?** eh lah meh-troh-poh-lee-<u>tah</u>-nah pehr…
Where are we?	**Dove siamo?** <u>doh</u>-veh <u>syah</u>-moh

▶ For ticketing, see page 19.

Boat and Ferry

When is the ferry to…?	**Quando parte il traghetto per…?** <u>kwahn</u>-doh <u>pahr</u>-teh eel trah-<u>gheht</u>-toh pehr…
Can I take my car?	**Posso portare l'auto?** <u>pohs</u>-soh pohr-<u>tah</u>-reh l-<u>ow</u>-toh

▶ For ticketing, see page 19.

You May See…

IMBARCAZIONE DI SALVATAGGIO	life boat
GIUBBOTTO DI SALVATAGGIO	life jacket

Genova, Livorno, Civitavecchia, Napoli, Messina and Reggio Calabria are the main ferry ports connecting the major and minor Italian islands. Travel along local coastal areas and lakes in Italy is enhanced by an extensive ferry system.

Bicycle and Motorcycle

I'd like to rent [hire]…	**Vorrei noleggiare…** vohr·<u>ray</u> noh·leh·<u>djah</u>·reh…
– a bicycle	**– una bici** <u>oo</u>·nah <u>bee</u>·chee
– a moped	**– uno scooter** <u>oo</u>·noh <u>skoo</u>·tehr
– a motorcycle	**– una moto** <u>oo</u>·nah <u>moh</u>·toh
How much per *day/week*?	**Qual è la tariffa per *un giorno/una settimana*?** kwah·<u>leh</u> lah tah·<u>reef</u>·fah pehr *oon jyohr·noh/<u>oo</u>·nah seht·tee·<u>mah</u>·nah*
Can I have a *helmet/lock*?	**Mi può dare un *casco/lucchetto*?** mee pwoh <u>dah</u>·reh oon *<u>kah</u>·skoh/look·<u>keht</u>·toh*

Taxi

Where can I get a taxi?	**Dove posso trovare un taxi?** <u>doh</u>·veh <u>pohs</u>·soh troh·<u>vah</u>·reh oon <u>tah</u>·ksee
I'd like a taxi *now/ for tomorrow at* (time)…	**Vorrei un taxi *subito/domani alle*…** vohr·<u>ray</u> oon <u>tah</u>·ksee *soo·<u>bee</u>·toh/doh·<u>mah</u>·nee <u>ahl</u>·leh*…
Pick me up at (place)…	**Venga a prendermi a…** <u>vehn</u>·gah ah <u>prehn</u>·dehr·mee ah…
I'm going to…	**Vado…** <u>vah</u>·doh…
– this address	**– a questo indirizzo** ah <u>kweh</u>·stoh een·dee·<u>ree</u>·tsoh
– the airport	**– all'aeroporto** ahl·lah·eh·roh·<u>pohr</u>·toh
– the train [railway] station	**– alla stazione ferroviaria** <u>ahl</u>·lah stah·<u>tsyoh</u>·neh fehr·roh·<u>vyah</u>·ryah
I'm late.	**Sono in ritardo.** <u>soh</u>·noh een ree·<u>tahr</u>·doh
Can you drive *faster/slower*?	**Può andare più *velocemente/lentamente*?** pwoh ahn·<u>dah</u>·reh pyoo *veh·loh·cheh·<u>mehn</u>·teh/ lehn·tah·<u>mehn</u>·teh*
Stop/Wait here.	***Si fermi/Mi aspetti* qui.** *see <u>fehr</u>·mee/mee ah·<u>speht</u>·tee* kwee

How much?	**Quant'è?** kwahn·<u>teh</u>
You said it would cost...	**Aveva detto che erano...** ah·<u>veh</u>·vah <u>deht</u>·toh keh <u>eh</u>·rah·noh...
Keep the change.	**Tenga il resto.** <u>tehn</u>·gah eel <u>reh</u>·stoh
A receipt, please.	**Una ricevuta, perfavore.** <u>oo</u>·nah ree·cheh·<u>voo</u>·tah pehr fah·<u>voh</u>·reh

Get a taxi at taxi stands or reserve by phone; hailing a taxi in the street is not common. Extra charges are added for travel at night (10 p.m.–7 a.m.), on Sundays and holidays, for extra luggage and for trips outside of town. Tip the driver by rounding off to the nearest euro or two.

Car

Car Rental [Hire]

Where's the car rental [hire]?	**Dov'è un autonoleggio?** doh·<u>veh</u> oon <u>ow</u>·toh·noh·<u>leh</u>·djoh
I'd like...	**Vorrei...** vohr·<u>ray</u>...
– a *cheap/small* car	– **un'auto *economica/piccola*** oo·<u>now</u>·toh eh·koh·<u>noh</u>·mee·kah/<u>peek</u>·koh·lah
– an automatic/ a manual	– **un'auto con il cambio *automatico/ manuale*** oo·<u>now</u>·toh kohn eel <u>kahm</u>·byoh <u>ow</u>·toh·<u>mah</u>·tee·koh/mah·<u>nwah</u>·leh
– air conditioning	– **un'auto con l'aria condizionata** oo·<u>now</u>·toh kohn <u>lah</u>·ryah kohn·dee·tsyoh·<u>nah</u>·tah
– a car seat	– **un sedile** oon seh·<u>dee</u>·leh
How much...?	**Qual è la tariffa...?** kwah·<u>leh</u> lah tah·<u>reef</u>·fah...
– per *day/week*	– **per *un giorno/una settimana*** pehr oon <u>jyohr</u>·noh/<u>oo</u>·nah seht·tee·<u>mah</u>·nah
– per kilometer	– **a chilometro** ah kee·<u>loh</u>·meh·troh
– for unlimited mileage	– **con chilometraggio illimitato** kohn kee·loh·meh·<u>trah</u>·djoh eel·lee·mee·<u>tah</u>·toh

31

Ha la patente internazionale? ah lah pah·<u>tehn</u>·teh een·tehr·nah·tsyoh·<u>nah</u>·leh

Do you have an international driver's license?

Il passaporto, per favore. eel pahs·sah·<u>pohr</u>·toh pehr fah·<u>voh</u>·reh

Your passport, please.

Desidera un'assicurazione supplementare? deh·<u>zee</u>·deh·rah oo·nah·see·koo·rah·<u>tsyoh</u>·neh soop·pleh·mehn·<u>tah</u>·reh

Do you want extra insurance?

Deve lasciare un deposito. <u>deh</u>·veh lah·<u>shah</u>·reh oon deh·<u>poh</u>·zee·toh

I'll need a deposit.

***Metta le iniziali/Firmi* qui.** <u>meht</u>·tah leh ee·nee·<u>tsyah</u>·lee/<u>feer</u>·mee kwee

Initial/Sign here.

Gas [Petrol] Station

Where's the gas [petrol] station?	**Dov'è un benzinaio?** doh·<u>veh</u> oon behn·dzee·<u>nah</u>·yoh
Fill it up.	**Faccia il pieno, per favore.** <u>fah</u>·chyah eel <u>pyeh</u>·noh pehr fah·<u>voh</u>·reh
...euros, please.	**...euro, per favore.** ...<u>eh</u>·oo·roh pehr fah·<u>voh</u>·reh
I'll pay *in cash/by credit card*.	**Pago *in contanti/con carta di credito*.** <u>pah</u>·goh *een kohn·<u>tahn</u>·tee/kohn <u>kahr</u>·tah dee <u>kreh</u>·dee·toh*

You May See...

SUPER	super
PREMIUM	premium
DIESEL	diesel

Asking Directions

Is this the way to…?	**Vado bene per…?** <u>vah</u>·doh <u>beh</u>·neh pehr…
How far is it to…?	**Quanto dista…?** <u>kwahn</u>·toh <u>dees</u>·tah…
Where's…?	**Dov'è…?** doh·<u>veh</u>…
–…Street	**– Via…** <u>vee</u>·ah…
– this address	**– questo indirizzo** <u>kweh</u>·stoh een·dee·<u>ree</u>·tsoh
– the highway [motorway]	**– l'autostrada** l·ow·toh·<u>strah</u>·dah
Can you show me on the map?	**Può indicarmelo sulla cartina?** pwoh een·dee·<u>kahr</u>·meh·loh <u>sool</u>·lah kahr·<u>tee</u>·nah
I'm lost.	**Mi sono perso♂/persa♀.** mee <u>soh</u>·noh <u>pehr</u>·soh♂/<u>pehr</u>·sah♀

You May Hear…

sempre dritto <u>sehm</u>·preh <u>dreet</u>·toh	straight ahead
a sinistra ah see·<u>nee</u>·strah	left
a destra ah <u>deh</u>·strah	right
all'angolo/dietro l'angolo ahl·<u>lahn</u>·goh·loh/<u>dyeh</u>·troh <u>lahn</u>·goh·loh	on the corner/around the corner
di fronte a dee <u>frohn</u>·teh ah	opposite
dietro a <u>dyeh</u>·troh ah	behind
accanto a ahk·<u>kahn</u>·toh ah	next to
dopo <u>doh</u>·poh	after
a *nord/sud* ah *nohrd/sood*	north/south
a *est/ovest* ah *ehst/<u>oh</u>·vehst*	east/west
al semaforo ahl seh·<u>mah</u>·foh·roh	at the traffic light
all'incrocio ahl·leen·<u>kroh</u>·chyoh	at the intersection

33

You May See...

 STOP — stop

 DARE LA PRECEDENZA — yield

 DIVIETO DI SOSTA — no parking

 CURVA PERICOLOSA — dangerous curve

 SENSO UNICO — one way

 STRADA CHIUSA — road closed

 DIVIETO DI SORPASSO — no passing

 DIVIETO DI INVERSIONE DI MARCIA — no u-turn

 Street parking in cities in limited; it's best to park in a **parcheggio** (parking lot or garage), day or night. Do not park in areas marked **Divieto di sosta** (no stopping except in emergency), **Divieto di fermata** (no stopping at any time) or **Passo carrabile** (do not block passageway).

Parking

Can I park here?	**Posso parcheggiare qui?** <u>pohs</u>·soh pahr·keh·<u>djah</u>·reh kwee
Where's the *parking lot [car park]/ parking meter*?	**Dov'è il *parcheggio/parchimetro*?** doh·<u>veh</u> eel pahr·<u>keh</u>·djoh/pahr·<u>kee</u>·meh·troh
How much...?	**Quanto costa...?** <u>kwahn</u>·toh <u>koh</u>·stah...
– per hour	**– all'ora** ahl·<u>loh</u>·rah
– per day	**– al giorno** ahl <u>jyohr</u>·noh
– for overnight	**– per tutta la notte** pehr <u>toot</u>·tah lah <u>noht</u>·teh

Breakdown and Repairs

My car *broke down/ won't start*.	**La mia auto *ha un'avaria al motore/ non parte*.** lah <u>mee</u>·ah <u>ow</u>·toh ah oo·nah·vah·<u>ree</u>·ah ahl moh·<u>toh</u>·reh/nohn <u>pahr</u>·teh
Can you fix it (today)?	**Può ripararla (oggi)?** pwoh ree·pah·<u>rahr</u>·lah (<u>oh</u>·djee)
When will it be ready?	**Per quando è pronta?** pehr <u>kwahn</u>·doh è <u>prohn</u>·tah
How much?	**Quanto mi costa?** <u>kwahn</u>·toh mee <u>koh</u>·stah

Accidents

There was an accident.	**C'è stato un incidente.** cheh <u>stah</u>·toh oon een·chee·<u>dehn</u>·teh
Call *an ambulance/ the police*.	**Chiami *un'ambulanza/la polizia*.** <u>kyah</u>·mee oo·nahm·boo·<u>lahn</u>·tsah/ lah poh·lee·<u>tsee</u>·ah

Essential

Can you recommend a hotel?	**Può consigliarmi un hotel?** pwoh kohn·see·<u>llyahr</u>·mee oon oh·<u>tehl</u>
I have a reservation.	**Ho una prenotazione.** oh <u>oo</u>·nah preh·noh·tah·<u>tsyoh</u>·neh
My name is…	**Mi chiamo…** mee <u>kyah</u>·moh…
Do you have a room…?	**Avete una camera…?** ah·<u>veh</u>·teh <u>oo</u>·nah <u>kah</u>·meh·rah…
– for one/two	**– singola/doppia** <u>seen</u>·goh·lah/<u>dohp</u>·pyah
– with a bathroom	**– con bagno** kohn <u>bah</u>·nyoh
– with air conditioning	**– con aria condizionata** kohn <u>ah</u>·ryah kohn·dee·tsyoh·<u>nah</u>·tah
For…	**Per…** pehr…
– tonight	**– stanotte** stah·<u>noht</u>·teh
– two nights	**– due notti** <u>doo</u>·eh <u>noht</u>·tee
– one week	**– una settimana** <u>oo</u>·nah seht·tee·<u>mah</u>·nah
How much?	**Quanto costa?** <u>kwahn</u>·toh <u>koh</u>·stah
Is there anything cheaper?	**C'è qualcosa di più economico?** cheh kwahl·<u>koh</u>·zah dee pyoo eh·koh·<u>noh</u>·mee·koh
When's check-out?	**A che ora devo lasciare la camera?** ah keh <u>oh</u>·rah <u>deh</u>·voh lah·<u>shah</u>·reh lah <u>kah</u>·meh·rah
Can I leave this in the safe?	**Posso lasciare questo nella cassaforte?** <u>pohs</u>·soh lah·<u>shah</u>·reh <u>kweh</u>·stoh <u>nehl</u>·lah kahs·sah·<u>fohr</u>·teh
Can I leave my bags?	**Posso lasciare le valigie?** <u>pohs</u>·soh lah·<u>shah</u>·reh leh vah·<u>lee</u>·jyeh

I'd like the bill/receipt.	**Vorrei *il conto/la ricevuta.*** vohr·ray *eel kohn·toh/lah ree·cheh·voo·tah*
I'll pay *in cash/ by credit card.*	**Pago *in contanti/con carta di credito.*** pah·goh *een kohn·tahn·tee/kohn kahr·tah dee kreh·dee·toh*

If you didn't reserve accommodations before your trip, visit the local **l'ufficio informazioni turistiche**, tourist information office, for recommendations on places to stay.

Finding Lodging

Can you recommend…?	**Può consigliarmi…?** pwoh kohn·see·llyahr·mee…
– a hotel	**– un hotel** oon oh·tehl
– a hostel	**– un ostello** oon oh·stehl·loh
– a campsite	**– un campeggio** oon kahm·peh·djoh
– a bed and breakfast	**– una pensione** oo·nah pehn·syoh·neh
What is it near?	**Vicino cosa c'è?** vee·chee·noh koh·zah cheh
How do I get there?	**Come ci si arriva?** koh·meh chee see ahr·ree·vah

A wide variety of accommodations is available in Italy, from budget to luxury. In recent years, **agriturismo** (farm-stays or ecotourism) have become very popular; these offer countryside locations, usually on a working farm, and often serve locally produced food. You may wish to stay in a **villa**, an upscale—and expensive—home or apartment, which often has a pool. **Una pensione** (bed and breakfast) is an ideal accommodation for budget-minded travelers who'd like to experience how Italians live. **Un hotel** can range in quality and price; many international chains have hotels throughout Italy.

At the Hotel

I have a reservation.	**Ho una prenotazione.** oh <u>oo</u>·nah preh·noh·tah·<u>tsyoh</u>·neh
My name is…	**Mi chiamo…** mee <u>kyah</u>·moh…
Do you have a room…?	**Avete una camera…?** ah·<u>veh</u>·teh <u>oo</u>·nah <u>kah</u>·meh·rah…
– with a *bathroom [toilet]/shower*	**– con *bagno/doccia*** kohn *<u>bah</u>·nyoh/ <u>doh</u>·chyah*
– with air conditioning	**– con aria condizionata** kohn <u>ah</u>·ryah kohn·dee·tsyoh·<u>nah</u>·tah
– that's *smoking/ non-smoking*	**– per *fumatori/non fumatori*** pehr *foo·mah·<u>toh</u>·ree/nohn foo·mah·<u>toh</u>·ree*
For…	**Per…** pehr…
– tonight	**– stanotte** stah·<u>noht</u>·teh
– two nights	**– due notti** <u>doo</u>·eh <u>noht</u>·tee
– a week	**– una settimana** <u>oo</u>·nah seht·tee·<u>mah</u>·nah

▶ For numbers, see page 177.

Do you have…?	**C'è…?** cheh…:
– a computer	**– un computer** oon kohm·<u>pyoo</u>·tehr
– an elevator [lift]	**– l'ascensore** lah·shehn·<u>soh</u>·reh
– (wireless) internet service	**– il collegamento Internet (wireless)** eel kohl·leh·gah·<u>mehn</u>·toh een·tehr·neht (<u>wyer</u>·lehs)
– room service	**– il servizio in camera** eel sehr·<u>vee</u>·tsyoh een <u>kah</u>·meh·rah
– a pool	**– la piscina** lah pee·<u>shee</u>·nah
– a gym	**– la palestra** lah pah·<u>leh</u>·strah
I need…	**Mi serve…** mee <u>sehr</u>·veh…
– an extra bed	**– un altro letto** oon <u>ahl</u>·troh <u>leht</u>·toh
– a cot	**– un lettino** oon leht·<u>tee</u>·noh
– a crib	**– una culla** <u>oo</u>·nah <u>kool</u>·lah

You May Hear…

Il suo passaporto/La sua carta di credito, per favore. eel <u>soo</u>·oh pahs·sah·<u>pohr</u>·toh/lah <u>soo</u>·ah <u>kahr</u>·tah dee <u>kreh</u>·dee·toh pehr fah·<u>voh</u>·reh

Your *passport/credit card*, please.

Compili questo modulo. kohm·<u>pee</u>·lee <u>kweh</u>·stoh <u>moh</u>·doo·loh

Fill out this form.

Firmi qui. <u>feer</u>·mee kwee

Sign here.

Price

How much per *day/week*?

Quanto costa *al giorno/alla settimana*? <u>kwahn</u>·toh <u>koh</u>·stah ahl <u>jyohr</u>·noh/<u>ahl</u>·lah seht·tee·<u>mah</u>·nah

Does that include *breakfast/sales tax [VAT]*?

La prima colazione/L'IVA è inclusa? lah <u>pree</u>·mah koh·lah·<u>tsyoh</u>·neh/<u>lee</u>·vah eh een·<u>kloo</u>·sah

Questions

Where's...?	**Dov'è...?** doh·<u>veh</u>...
– the bar	**– il bar** eel bahr
– the bathroom [toilet]	**– la toilette** lah <u>twah</u>·leht
– the elevator [lift]	**– l'ascensore** lah·shehn·<u>soh</u>·reh
Can I have...?	**Può darmi...?** pwoh <u>dahr</u>·mee...
– a blanket	**– una coperta** <u>oo</u>·nah koh·<u>pehr</u>·tah
– an iron	**– un ferro da stiro** oon <u>fehr</u>·roh dah <u>stee</u>·roh
– a pillow	**– un cuscino** oon koo·<u>shee</u>·noh
– soap	**– una saponetta** <u>oo</u>·nah sah·poh·<u>neht</u>·tah
– toilet paper	**– della carta igienica** <u>dehl</u>·lah <u>kahr</u>·tah ee·<u>jyeh</u>·nee·kah
– a towel	**– un asciugamano** oon ah·shoo·gah·<u>mah</u>·noh
Do you have an adapter for this?	**Avete un adattatore?** ah·<u>veh</u>·teh oon ah·daht·toh·<u>tohr</u>·eh
How do I turn on the lights?	**Come si accendono le luci?** <u>koh</u>·meh see ah·<u>chehn</u>·doh·noh leh <u>loo</u>·chee
Can you wake me at...?	**Può svegliarmi alle...?** pwoh zveh·<u>llyahr</u>·mee <u>ahl</u>·leh...
Can I leave this in the safe?	**Posso lasciare questo nella cassaforte?** <u>pohs</u>·soh lah·<u>shah</u>·reh <u>kweh</u>·stoh <u>nehl</u>·lah kahs·sah·<u>fohr</u>·teh
Can I have my things from the safe?	**Posso prendere le mie cose dalla cassaforte?** <u>pohs</u>·soh <u>prehn</u>·deh·reh leh mee·<u>eh</u> <u>koh</u>·zeh <u>dahl</u>·lah kahs·sah·<u>fohr</u>·teh
Is there *mail [post]/ a message* for me?	***C'è posta/Ci sono messaggi* per me?** cheh <u>poh</u>·stah/chee <u>soh</u>·noh mehs·<u>sah</u>·djee pehr meh

You May See...

SPINGERE/TIRARE	push/pull
TOILETTE	bathroom [toilet]
DOCCIA	shower
ASCENSORE	elevator [lift]
SCALE	stairs
LAVANDERIA	laundry
NON DISTURBARE	do not disturb
PORTA ANTINCENDIO	fire door
USCITA (D'EMERGENZA)	(emergency) exit
SERVIZIO SVEGLIA	wake-up call

Problems

There's a problem.	**C'è un problema.** cheh oon proh·*bleh*·mah
I lost my *key/key card*.	**Ho perso la *chiave/chiave elettronica*.** oh *pehr*·soh lah *kyah·veh/kyah·veh eh·leht·troh·nee·kah*
I'm locked out of the room.	**Sono rimasto chiuso♂/rimasta chiusa♀ fuori.** *soh*·noh ree·*mah*·stoh kyoo·zoh♂/ ree·*mah*·stah kyoo·zah♀ *fwoh*·ree
There's no *hot water/toilet paper.*	**Non c'è *acqua calda/carta igienica*.** nohn cheh *ah*·kwah *kahl*·dah/*kahr*·tah ee·*jyeh*·nee·kah
The room is dirty.	**La camera è sporca.** lah *kah*·meh·rah eh *spohr*·kah
There are bugs in the room.	**In camera ci sono degli insetti.** een *kah*·meh·rah chee *soh*·noh *deh*·llyee een·*seht*·tee
The...doesn't work.	**...non funziona.** ...nohn foon·*tsyoh*·nah

Can you fix…?	**Può riparare…?** pwoh ree·pah·<u>rah</u>·reh…
– the air conditioning	**– l'aria condizionata** <u>lah</u>·ryah kohn·dee·tsyoh·<u>nah</u>·tah
– the fan	**– il ventilatore** eel vehn·tee·lah·<u>toh</u>·reh
– the heat [heating]	**– il riscaldamento** eel ree·skahl·dah·<u>mehn</u>·toh
– the light	**– la luce** lah <u>loo</u>·cheh
– the TV	**– la TV** lah tee·<u>voo</u>
– the toilet	**– il gabinetto** eel gah·bee·<u>neht</u>·toh
I'd like another room.	**Vorrei un'altra camera.** vohr·<u>ray</u> oo·<u>nahl</u>·trah <u>kah</u>·meh·rah

Voltage is 220–240V, and plugs are two-pronged. You may need a converter and/or an adapter for your appliances.

Check-out

When's check-out?	**A che ora devo lasciare la camera?** ah keh <u>oh</u>·rah <u>deh</u>·voh lah·<u>shah</u>·reh lah <u>kah</u>·meh·rah
Can I leave my bags here until…?	**Posso lasciare le valigie fino alle…?** <u>pohs</u>·soh lah·<u>shah</u>·reh leh vah·<u>lee</u>·jyeh <u>fee</u>·noh <u>ahl</u>·leh…
Can I have an itemized *bill/receipt*?	**Posso avere *il conto dettagliato/la ricevuta*?** <u>pohs</u>·soh ah·<u>veh</u>·reh eel <u>kohn</u>·toh deht·tah·<u>llyah</u>·toh/lah ree·cheh·<u>voo</u>·tah
I think there's a mistake.	**Credo che ci sia un errore.** <u>kreh</u>·doh keh chee <u>see</u>·ah oon ehr·<u>roh</u>·reh
I'll pay *in cash/by credit card*.	**Pago *in contanti/con carta di credito*.** pah·ghoh een kohn·<u>tahn</u>·tee/kohn <u>kahr</u>·tah dee <u>kreh</u>·dee·toh

A service fee is generally included in bills throughout Italy. It's optional to tip porters and housekeeping staff, though a tip for good service is always appreciated. Your concierge will appreciate a tip for any helpful services provided.

Renting

I reserved *an apartment/a room.*
Ho prenotato *un appartamento/una camera.*
oh preh·noh·*tah*·toh oon ahp·pahr·tah·*mehn*·toh/
oo·nah *kah*·meh·rah

My name is...
Mi chiamo... mee kyah·moh...

Can I have the *key/key card*?
Mi può dare la *chiave/chiave elettronica*?
mee pwoo *dah*·reh lah *kyah*·veh/ kyah·veh
eh·leht·*troh*·nee·kah

Are there...?
Ci sono...? chee soh·noh...

– dishes
– **i piatti** ee *pyaht*·tee

– pillows
– **i cuscini** ee koo·*shee*·nee

– sheets
– **le lenzuola** leh lehn·*tswoh*·lah

– towels
– **gli asciugamani** llyee ah·shoo·gah·*mah*·nee

– utensils
– **gli utensili** llyee oo·*tehn*·see·lee

When do I put out the *trash [rubbish]/ recycling*?
Quando si mette fuori il secchio *della spazzatura/il riciclaggio*?
kwahn·doh see *meht*·teh *fwoh*·ree eel *sehk*·kyoh *dehl*·lah spah·tsah·*too*·rah/eel ree·chee·*klah*·djoh

...is broken.
...non funziona. ...nohn foon·*tsyoh*·nah

How does...work?
Come funziona...? *koh*·meh foon·*tsyoh*·nah...

– the air conditioner
– **il condizionatore** eel kohn·dee·tsyoh·nah·*toh*·reh

– the dishwasher
– **la lavastoviglie** lah lah·vah·stoh·*vee*·llyeh

– the freezer
– **il freezer** eel *free*·zehr

– the heater
– **il riscaldamento** eel ree·skahl·dah·*mehn*·toh

– the microwave
– **il microonde** eel mee·kroh·*ohn*·deh

– the refrigerator
– **il frigo** eel *free*·goh

– the stove
– **la cucina** lah koo·*chee*·nah

– the washing machine
– **la lavatrice** lah lah·vah·*tree*·cheh

Household Items

I need...	**Ho bisogno di...** oh bee·soh·nyoh dee...
– an adapter	– **un adattatore** oon ah·daht·toh·toh·reh
– aluminum [kitchen] foil	– **carta stagnola** kahr·tah stah·nyoh·lah
– a bottle opener	– **un apribottiglie** oon ah·pree·boht·tee·llyeh
– a broom	– **una scopa** oo·nah skoh·pah
– a can opener	– **un apriscatole** oon ah·pree·skah·toh·leh
– cleaning supplies	– **prodotti per le pulizie** proh·doht·tee pehr leh poo·lee·tsee·eh
– a corkscrew	– **un cavatappi** oon kah·vah·tahp·pee
– detergent	– **detersivo** deh·tehr·see·voh
– dishwashing liquid	– **detersivo per i piatti** deh·tehr·see·voh pehr ee pyaht·tee
– garbage [rubbish] bags	– **sacchetti per i rifiuti** sahk·keht·tee pehr ee ree·fyoo·tee
– a lightbulb	– **una lampadina** oo·nah lahm·pah·dee·nah
– matches	– **fiammiferi** fyahm·mee·feh·ree
– a mop	– **un mocio** oon moh·choh
– napkins	– **tovaglioli** toh·vah·llyoh·lee
– paper towels	– **carta da cucina** kahr·tah dah koo·chee·nah
– plastic wrap [cling film]	– **pellicola per alimenti** pehl·lee·koh·lah pehr ah·lee·mehn·tee
– a plunger	– **uno sturalavandini** oo·noh stoo·rah·lah·vahn·dee·nee

44

– scissors	– **un paio di forbici** oon <u>pah</u>·yoh dee <u>fohr</u>·bee·chee
– a vacuum cleaner	– **un aspirapolvere** oon ah·spee·rah·<u>pohl</u>·veh·reh

▶ For dishes and utensils, see page 65.

▶ For oven temperatures, see page 183.

Hostel

Is there a bed available?	**C'è un letto disponibile?** cheh oon <u>leht</u>·toh dee·spoh·<u>nee</u>·bee·leh
Can I have…?	**Potrei avere…?** poh·<u>tray</u> ah·<u>veh</u>·reh
– a *single/double* room	– **una camera *singola/doppia*** <u>oo</u>·nah <u>kah</u>·meh·rah <u>seen</u>·goh·lah/<u>dohp</u>·pyah
– a blanket	– **una coperta** <u>oo</u>·nah koh·<u>pehr</u>·tah
– a pillow	– **un cuscino** oon koo·<u>shee</u>·noh
– sheets	– **delle lenzuola** <u>dehl</u>·leh lehn·<u>tswoh</u>·lah
– a towel	– **un asciugamano** oon ah·shoo·gah·<u>mah</u>·noh
When do you lock up?	**A che ora chiudete?** ah keh <u>oh</u>·rah kyoo·<u>deh</u>·teh

i

Hostels are inexpensive accommodations that have dormitory-style sleeping arrangements and private or semi-private rooms. Some hostels have rooms with private bathrooms, though most offer shared bathrooms. There is usually a self-service kitchen on-site. Reservations are recommended in advance in larger cities and popular tourist destinations during the tourist season. Visit the Hostelling International website for details.

Camping

Can I camp here?	**Si può campeggiare?** see pwoh kahm‧peh‧<u>djah</u>‧reh
Where's the campsite?	**Dov'è il campeggio?** doh‧<u>veh</u> eel kahm‧<u>peh</u>‧djoh
What is the charge per *day/week*?	**Qual è la tariffa per *un giorno/una settimana*?** kwah‧<u>leh</u> lah tah‧<u>reef</u>‧fah pehr *oon jyohr‧noh/<u>oo</u>‧nah seht‧tee‧<u>mah</u>‧nah*
Are there...?	**Ci sono...?** chee <u>soh</u>‧noh...
– cooking facilities	**– le attrezzature per cucinare** leh aht‧treh‧tsah‧<u>too</u>‧reh pehr koo‧chee‧<u>nah</u>‧reh
– electric outlets	**– le prese elettriche** leh <u>preh</u>‧seh eh‧<u>leht</u>‧tree‧keh
– laundry facilities	**– le lavanderie** leh lah‧vahn‧deh‧<u>ree</u>‧eh
– showers	**– le docce** leh <u>doh</u>‧cheh
– tents for rent [hire]	**– tende a noleggio** <u>tehn</u>‧deh ah noh‧<u>leh</u>‧djoh
Where can I empty the chemical toilet?	**Dove posso vuotare il water?** <u>doh</u>‧veh <u>pohs</u>‧soh vwoh‧<u>tah</u>‧reh eel <u>vah</u>‧tchr

You May See...

ACQUA POTABILE	drinking water
NO CAMPING	no camping
DIVIETO DI *FALÒ/BARBECUE*	no *fires/barbecues*

▶ For household items, see page 44.

▶ For dishes and utensils, see page 65.

Essential

Where's an internet cafe?	**Dov'è un Internet caffè?** doh·<u>veh</u> oon <u>een</u>·tehr·neht kahf·<u>feh</u>
Can I *access the internet/check e-mail*?	**Posso *collegarmi a Internet/controllare le e-mail*?** <u>pohs</u>·soh kohl·leh·<u>gahr</u>·mee ah <u>een</u>·tehr·neht/kohn·trohl·<u>lah</u>·reh leh <u>ee</u>·mayl
How much per *hour/half hour*?	**Quanto costa per *un'ora/mezz'ora*?** <u>kwahn</u>·toh <u>koh</u>·stah pehr *oon·<u>oh</u>·rah/ mehdz·<u>oh</u>·rah*
How do I log on?	**Come si fa il login?** <u>koh</u>·meh see fah eel loh·<u>geen</u>
A phone card, please.	**Una scheda telefonica, per favore.** <u>oo</u>·nah <u>skeh</u>·dah teh·leh·<u>foh</u>·nee·kah pehr fah·<u>voh</u>·reh
Can I have your number, please?	**Mi può dare il suo numero, per favore?** mee pwoh <u>dah</u>·reh eel <u>soo</u>·oh <u>noo</u>·meh·roh pehr fah·<u>voh</u>·reh
Here's my *number/e-mail*.	**Ecco *il mio numero/la mia e-mail*.** <u>ehk</u>·koh *eel <u>mee</u>·oh <u>noo</u>·meh·roh/lah <u>mee</u>·ah <u>ee</u>·mayl*
Call/E-mail me.	**Mi *chiami/mandi* una e-mail.** mee <u>kyah</u>·mee/<u>mahn</u>·dee <u>oo</u>·nah <u>ee</u>·mayl
Hello. This is...	**Pronto. Sono...** <u>prohn</u>·toh <u>soh</u>·noh...
Can I speak to...?	**Posso parlare con...?** <u>pohs</u>·soh pahr·<u>lah</u>·reh kohn...
Can you repeat that?	**Può ripetere?** pwoh ree·<u>peh</u>·teh·reh
I'll call back later.	**Richiamo più tardi.** ree·<u>kyah</u>·moh pyoo <u>tahr</u>·dee
Bye.	**Arrivederla.** ahr·ree·veh·<u>dehr</u>·lah
Where's the post office?	**Dov'è un ufficio postale?** doh·<u>veh</u> oon oof·<u>fee</u>·chyoh poh·<u>stah</u>·leh
I'd like to send this to...	**Vorrei inviare questo a...** vohr·<u>ray</u> een·<u>vyah</u>·reh <u>kweh</u>·stoh ah...

Computer, Internet and E-mail

Where's an internet cafe?	**Dov'è un Internet caffè?** doh-<u>veh</u> oon <u>een</u>-tehr-neht kahf-<u>feh</u>
Does it have wireless internet?	**C'è il wireless?** cheh eel <u>wyehr</u>-lehs
How do I turn the computer *on/off*?	**Come si *accende/spegne* il computer?** <u>koh</u>-meh see ah-<u>chehn</u>-deh/<u>speh</u>-nyeh eel kohm-<u>pyoo</u>-tehr
Can I...?	**Posso...?** <u>pohs</u>-soh...
– access the internet	– **collegarmi (a Internet)** kohl-leh-<u>gahr</u>-mee (ah <u>een</u>-tehr-neht)
– check e-mail	– **controllare le e-mail** kohn-trohl-<u>lah</u>-reh leh <u>ee</u>-mayl
– print	– **stampare** stahm-<u>pah</u>-reh
How much *per hour/half hour*?	**Quanto costa per un'ora/mezz'ora?** <u>kwahn</u>-toh <u>koh</u>-stah pehr *oon-<u>oh</u>-rah/ mehdz-<u>oh</u>-rah*
How do I...?	**Come...?** <u>koh</u>-meh...
– connect/disconnect	– **ci si *collega/scollega*** chee see *kohl-<u>leh</u>-gah/skohl-<u>leh</u>-gah*
– log on/log off	– **si fa il *login/logout*** see fah eel loh-<u>geen</u>/loh-<u>gowt</u>
– type this symbol	– **digiti questo simbolo** <u>dee</u>-jee-tee <u>kweh</u>-stoh <u>seem</u>-boh-loh
What's your e-mail?	**Qual è la sua e-mail?** kwahl-<u>eh</u> lah <u>soo</u>-ah <u>ee</u>-mayl
My e-mail is...	**La mia e-mail è...** lah <u>mee</u>-ah <u>ee</u>-mayl eh...

You May See...

CHIUDI	close
ELIMINA	delete
E-MAIL	e-mail
ESCI	exit
AIUTO	help
INSTANT MESSENGER	instant messenger
INTERNET	internet
LOGIN	login
NUOVO (MESSAGGIO)	new (message)
ACCESSO/SPENTO	on/off
APRI	open
STAMPA	print
SALVA	save
INVIA	send
NOME UTENTE/PASSWORD	username/password
WIRELESS	wireless internet

Phone

A phone card, please.	**Una scheda telefonica, per favore.** oo·nah skeh·dah teh·leh·<u>foh</u>·nee·kah pehr fah·<u>voh</u>·reh
How much?	**Quant'è?** kwahn·<u>teh</u>
My phone doesn't work here.	**Il telefonino non prende.** eel teh·leh·foh·nee·noh nohn <u>prehn</u>·deh
What's the *area code/country code* for…?	**Qual è il *prefisso/prefisso internazionale* per…?** kwahl eh eel *preh·<u>fees</u>·soh/ preh·<u>fees</u>·soh een·tehr·nah·tsyoh·<u>nah</u>·leh* pehr…
What's the number for Information?	**Che numero ha il servizio informazioni?** keh <u>noo</u>·meh·roh ah eel sehr·<u>vee</u>·tsyoh een·fohr·mah·<u>tsyoh</u>·nee
I'd like the number for…	**Vorrei il numero *di/del/della/dell'*…** vohr·<u>ray</u> eel <u>noo</u>·meh·roh pehr *dee/dehl/ dehl·lah/dehl*…

▶For when to use **di/del/della/dell'**, see page 174.

Can I have your number, please?	**Mi può dare il suo numero, per favore?** mee pwoh <u>dah</u>·reh eel <u>soo</u>·oh <u>noo</u>·meh·roh pehr fah·<u>voh</u>·reh
Here's my number.	**Ecco il mio numero.** <u>ehk</u>·koh eel <u>mee</u>·oh <u>noo</u>·meh·roh

▶For numbers, see page 177.

Call/Text me.	**Mi *chiami/mandi* un SMS.** mee <u>kyah</u>·mee/ <u>mahn</u>·dee oon <u>ehs</u>·seh <u>ehm</u>·meh <u>ehs</u>·seh
I'll call you.	**La chiamo.** lah <u>kyah</u>·moh
I'll text you.	**Le mando un SMS.** leh <u>mahn</u>·doh oon <u>ehs</u>·seh <u>ehm</u>·meh <u>ehs</u>·seh

On the Phone

Hello. This is…	**Pronto. Sono…** <u>prohn</u>·toh <u>soh</u>·noh…
Can I speak to…?	**Posso parlare con…?** <u>pohs</u>·soh pahr·<u>lah</u>·reh kohn…
Extension…	**Interno…** een·<u>tehr</u>·noh…
Speak *louder/more slowly*, please.	**Parli più *forte/lentamente*, per favore.** <u>pahr</u>·lee pyoo *<u>fohr</u>·teh/lehn·tah·<u>mehn</u>·teh* pehr fah·<u>voh</u>·reh
Can you repeat that?	**Può ripetere?** pwoh ree·<u>peh</u>·teh·reh
I'll call back later.	**Richiamo più tardi.** ree·<u>kyah</u>·moh pyoo <u>tahr</u>·dee
Bye.	**Arrivederla.** ahr·ree·veh·<u>dehr</u>·lah

▶ For business travel, see page 149.

You May Hear…

Chi parla? kee <u>pahr</u>·lah	Who's calling?
Attenda. aht·<u>tehn</u>·dah	Hold on.
Le passo il numero. leh <u>pahs</u>·soh eel <u>noo</u>·meh·roh	I'll put you through.
Non c'è. nohn cheh	He/She is not here.
È al telefono. eh ahl teh·<u>leh</u>·foh·noh	He/She is on another line.
Vuole lasciare un messaggio? <u>vwoh</u>·leh lah·<u>shah</u>·reh oon mehs·<u>sah</u>·djoh	Would you like to leave a message?
Richiami *più tardi/fra dieci minuti*. ree·<u>kyah</u>·mee *pyoo <u>tahr</u>·dee/frah <u>dyeh</u>·chee mee·<u>noo</u>·tee*	Call back *later/in 10 minutes*.
Può richiamarla? pwoh ree·kyah·<u>mahr</u>·lah	Can he/she call you back?
Mi lascia il suo numero? mee <u>lah</u>·shah eel <u>soo</u>·oh <u>noo</u>·meh·roh	What's your number?

Fax

Can I *send/receive* a fax here?	**Posso *inviare/ricevere* un fax?** pohs·soh *een·vyah·reh/ree·cheh·veh·reh* oon fahks
What's the fax number?	**Qual è il numero di fax?** kwahl·eh eel noo·meh·roh dee fahks
Please fax this to…	**Invii questo fax a…, per favore.** een·vee·ee kweh·stoh fahks ah…pehr fah·voh·reh

---

i Most public phones are card-operated; phone cards can be purchased at **edicole** (newsstands), **caffè** (coffee bars) and **tabacchi** (tobacconists). For international calls, calling cards are the most economical. Calling internationally from your hotel may be convenient, but the rates can be very expensive.

To call the U.S. or Canada from Italy, dial 00 + 1 + area code + phone number. To call the U.K. from Italy, dial 00 + 44 + area code (minus the first 0) + phone number.

To make a local or national call within Italy, dial the area code then the phone number. A list of codes can be found in the phone book.

Post Office

| Where's the *post office/mailbox [postbox]*? | **Dov'è *un ufficio postale/una buca delle lettere*?** doh·veh oon oof·fee·chyoh poh·stah·leh/oo·nah boo·kah dehl·leh leht·teh·reh |
| A stamp for this *postcard/letter* to… | **Un francobollo per questa *cartolina/ lettera* per…** oon frahn·koh·bohl·loh pehr kweh·stah kahr·toh·lee·nah/leht·teh·rah pehr… |

How much?	**Quant'è?** kwahn·<u>teh</u>
Send this package by airmail/express.	**Mandi questo pacco *per posta aerea/espresso.*** <u>mahn</u>·dee <u>kweh</u>·stoh <u>pahk</u>·koh *pehr <u>poh</u>·stah ah·<u>eh</u>·reh·ah/eh·<u>sprehs</u>·soh*
A receipt, please.	**La ricevuta, per favore.** lah ree·cheh·<u>voo</u>·tah pehr fah·<u>voh</u>·reh

You May Hear…

Riempia il modulo per la dogana. <u>ryehm</u>·pee·ah eel <u>moh</u>·doo·loh pehr lah doh·<u>gah</u>·nah	Fill out the customs declaration form.
Valore? vah·<u>loh</u>·reh	What's the value?
Cosa c'è dentro? <u>koh</u>·zah cheh <u>dehn</u>·troh	What's inside?

i **Gli uffici postali** (post offices) are open Monday through Friday 8:30 a.m.–6:30 p.m. and Saturday from 8:30 a.m.–12:30 p.m. If you need to send valuable items, choose **posta raccomandata** (registered mail). Stamps can also be purchased at **tabacchi** (tobacconists).

▼ Food

Essential

Can you recommend a good *restaurant/ bar*?	**Può consigliarmi un buon *ristorante/bar*?** pwoh kohn·see·<u>llyahr</u>·mee oon bwohn *ree·stoh·<u>rahn</u>·teh/bahr*
Is there *a traditional/ an inexpensive* restaurant nearby?	**C'è un ristorante *tipico/economico* qui vicino?** cheh oon ree·stoh·<u>rahn</u>·teh *<u>tee</u>·pee·koh/eh·koh·<u>noh</u>·mee·koh* kwee vee·<u>chee</u>·noh
A table for…, please.	**Un tavolo per…, per favore.** oon <u>tah</u>·voh·loh pehr…pehr fah·<u>voh</u>·reh
Can we sit…?	**Possiamo sederci…?** pohs·<u>syah</u>·moh seh·<u>dehr</u>·chee…
– here/there	**– qui/là** kwee/lah
– outside	**– fuori** <u>fwoh</u>·ree
– in a (non-) smoking area	**– in una sala per (non) fumatori** een <u>oo</u>·nah sah·lah pehr (nohn) foo·mah·<u>toh</u>·ree
I'm waiting for someone.	**Sto aspettando qualcuno.** stoh ah·speht·<u>tahn</u>·doh kwahl·<u>koo</u>·noh
Where's the restroom [toilet]?	**Dov'è la toilette?** doh·<u>veh</u> lah <u>twah</u>·leht
The menu, please.	**Il menù, per favore.** eel meh·<u>noo</u> pehr fah·<u>voh</u>·reh
What do you recommend?	**Cosa mi consiglia?** <u>koh</u>·zah mee kohn·<u>see</u>·llyah
I'd like…	**Vorrei…** vohr·<u>ray</u>…
Enjoy your meal!	**Buon appetito!** bwohn ahp·peh·<u>tee</u>·toh
The check [bill], please.	**Il conto, per favore.** eel <u>kohn</u>·toh pehr fah·<u>voh</u>·reh

Is service included?	**Il servizio è compreso?** eel sehr·<u>vee</u>·tsyoh eh kohm·<u>preh</u>·zoh
Can I *pay by credit card/have a receipt*?	**Posso *pagare con carta di credito/avere una ricevuta*?** <u>pohs</u>·soh pah·<u>gah</u>·reh kohn <u>kahr</u>·tah dee <u>kreh</u>·dee·toh/ah·<u>veh</u>·reh <u>oo</u>·nah ree·cheh·<u>voo</u>·tah
Thank you!	**Grazie!** <u>grah</u>·tsyeh

Restaurant Types

Can you recommend…?	**Può consigliarmi…?** pwoh kohn·see·<u>llyahr</u>·mee…
– a restaurant	**– un ristorante** oon ree·stoh·<u>rahn</u>·teh
– a bar	**– un bar** oon bahr
– a cafe	**– un caffè** oon kahf·<u>feh</u>
– a fast-food place	**– un fast food** oon fahst food
– a pizzeria	**– una pizzeria** <u>oo</u>·nah pee·tseh·<u>ree</u>·ah

La prima colazione (breakfast) is typically espresso or cappuccino with a croissant or sweet pastry. **Il pranzo** (lunch) is served between 12 p.m. and 2 p.m. and is usually the main meal of the day. **La cena** (dinner) is served between 7 p.m. and 10 p.m. **Le merende** (snacks) are popular at mid-morning or mid-afternoon; these include a sweet pastry, ice cream or small pizza.

Reservations and Questions

I'd like to reserve a table…	**Vorrei prenotare un tavolo…** vohr·<u>ray</u> preh·noh·<u>tah</u>·reh oon <u>tah</u>·voh·loh…
– for two	**– per due** pehr <u>doo</u>·eh
– for this evening	**– per questa sera** pehr <u>kweh</u>·stah <u>seh</u>·rah
– for tomorrow at…	**– per domani alle…** pehr doh·<u>mah</u>·nee <u>ahl</u>·leh…
A table for two, please.	**Un tavolo per due, per favore.** oon <u>tah</u>·voh·loh pehr <u>doo</u>·eh pehr fah·<u>voh</u>·reh
We have a reservation.	**Abbiamo prenotato.** ahb·<u>byah</u>·moh preh·noh·<u>tah</u>·toh
My name is…	**Mi chiamo…** mee <u>kyah</u>·moh…
Can we sit…?	**Possiamo sederci…** pohs·<u>syah</u>·moh seh·<u>dehr</u>·chee…
– here/there	**– qui/là** kwee/lah
– outside	**– fuori** <u>fwoh</u>·ree
– in a (non-) smoking area	**– in una sala per (non) fumatori** een <u>oo</u>·nah <u>sah</u>·lah pehr (nohn) foo·mah·<u>toh</u>·ree
– by the window	**– vicino alla finestra** vee·<u>chee</u>·noh <u>ahl</u>·lah fee·<u>neh</u>·strah
Where's the restroom [toilet]?	**Dov'è la toilette?** doh·<u>veh</u> lah <u>twah</u>·leht

Ha prenotato?
ah preh·noh·<u>tah</u>·toh

Do you have
a reservation?

Per quante persone?
pehr <u>kwahn</u>·teh pehr·<u>soh</u>·neh

How many?

Volete ordinare?
voh·<u>leh</u>·teh ohr·dee·<u>nah</u>·reh

Are you ready to
order?

Che cosa desidera?
keh <u>koh</u>·zah deh·<u>zee</u>·deh·rah

What would you like?

Le consiglio...
leh kohn·<u>see</u>·llyoh...

I recommend...

Buon appetito.
bwohn ahp·peh·<u>tee</u>·toh

Enjoy your meal.

Ordering

Excuse me!	**Scusi!** <u>skooh</u>·see
We're ready to order.	**Vorremmo ordinare.** vohr·<u>rehm</u>·moh ohr·dee·<u>nah</u>·reh
The wine list, please.	**La carta dei vini, per favore.** lah <u>kahr</u>·tah day <u>vee</u>·nee pehr fah·<u>voh</u>·reh
I'd like...	**Vorrei...** vohr·<u>ray</u>...
– a bottle of...	**– una bottiglia di...** <u>oo</u>·nah boht·<u>tee</u>·llyah dee...
– a carafe of...	**– una caraffa di...** <u>oo</u>·nah kah·<u>rahf</u>·fah dee...
– a glass of...	**– un bicchiere di...** oon beek·<u>kyeh</u>·reh dee...

▶ For alcoholic and non-alcoholic drinks, see page 85.

The menu, please.	**Il menù, per favore.** eel meh·<u>noo</u> pehr fah·<u>voh</u>·reh
Do you have…?	**Avete…?** ah·<u>veh</u>·teh…
– a menu in English	**– un menù in inglese** oon meh·<u>noo</u> een een·<u>gleh</u>·zeh
– a fixed-price menu	**– un menù a prezzo fisso** oon meh·<u>noo</u> ah <u>preh</u>·tsoh <u>fees</u>·soh
– a children's menu	**– un menù per bambini** oon meh·<u>noo</u> pehr bahm·<u>bee</u>·nee
What do you recommend?	**Cosa mi consiglia?** <u>koh</u>·zah mee kohn·<u>see</u>·llyah
What's this?	**Questo che cos'è?** <u>kweh</u>·stoh keh koh·<u>zeh</u>
What's in it?	**Cosa c'è dentro?** <u>koh</u>·zah cheh <u>dehn</u>·troh
Is it spicy?	**È piccante?** eh peek·<u>kahn</u>·teh
Without…, please.	**Senza…, per favore.** <u>sehn</u>·tsah…pehr fah·<u>voh</u>·reh
It's to go [take away].	**È da portare via.** eh dah pohr·<u>tahr</u>·eh <u>vee</u>·ah

You May See…

COPERTO	cover charge
PREZZO FISSO	fixed-price
MENÙ	menu
MENÙ DEL GIORNO	menu of the day
SERVIZIO (NON) COMPRESO	service (not) included
SPECIALITÀ DEL GIORNO	daily specials

Cooking Methods

baked	**al forno** ahl <u>fohr</u>·noh
boiled	**lesso** <u>lehs</u>·soh
braised	**brasato** brah·<u>zah</u>·toh
breaded	**impanato** eem·pah·<u>nah</u>·toh
creamed	**passato** pahs·<u>sah</u>·toh
diced	**a cubetti** ah koo·<u>beht</u>·tee
filleted	**filetto** fee·<u>leht</u>·toh
fried	**fritto** <u>freet</u>·toh
grilled	**grigliato** gree·<u>llyah</u>·toh
poached	**in bianco** een <u>byahn</u>·koh
roasted	**arrosto** ahr·<u>roh</u>·stoh
sautéed	**saltato** sahl·<u>tah</u>·toh
smoked	**affumicato** ahf·foo·mee·<u>kah</u>·toh
steamed	**al vapore** ahl vah·<u>poh</u>·reh
stewed	**stufato** stoo·<u>fah</u>·toh
stuffed	**ripieno** ree·<u>pyeh</u>·noh

Special Requirements

I'm...	**Sono...** <u>soh</u>·noh...
– diabetic	**– diabetico**♂**/diabetica**♀ dyah·<u>beh</u>·tee·koh♂/ dyah·<u>beh</u>·tee·kah♂
– lactose intolerant	**– intollerante al lattosio** een·tohl·leh·<u>rahn</u>·teh ahl laht·<u>toh</u>·syoh
– vegetarian	**– vegetariano**♂**/vegetariana**♀ veh·jeh·tah·<u>ryah</u>·noh♂/veh·jeh·tah·<u>ryah</u>·nah♀
I'm allergic to...	**Sono allergico**♂**/allergica**♀ **a...** <u>soh</u>·noh ahl·<u>lehr</u>·jee·koh♂/ ahl·<u>lehr</u>·jee·kah♀ ah...

I can't eat…	**Non posso mangiare…** nohn pohs·soh mahn·_jyah_·reh…
– dairy	**– i latticini** ee laht·tee·_chee_·nee
– gluten	**– il glutine** eel _gloo_·tee·neh
– nuts	**– le noci** leh _noh_·chee
– pork	**– il maiale** eel mah·_yah_·leh
– shellfish	**– i frutti di mare** ee _froot_·tee dee _mah_·reh
– spicy foods	**– i cibi piccanti** ee _chee_·bee peek·_kahn_·tee
– wheat	**– il grano** eel _grah_·noh
Is it kosher?	**È kosher?** eh _koh_·shehr

Dining with Kids

Do you have children's portions?	**Ci sono porzioni per bambini?** chee _soh_·noh pohr·_tsyoh_·nee pehr bahm·_bee_·nee
A *highchair/child's seat*, please.	**Un *seggiolone/seggiolino* da bambino, per favore.** oon seh·djoh·_loh_·neh/ seh·djoh·_lee_·noh dah bahm·_bee_·noh pehr fah·_voh_·reh
Where can I *feed/ change* the baby?	**Dove posso *dare da mangiare al/cambiare il* bambino?** _doh_·veh pohs·soh _dah_·reh dah mahn·_jyah_·reh ahl/kahm·_byah_·reh eel bahm·_bee_·noh
Can you warm this?	**Me lo può scaldare?** meh loh pwoh skahl·_dah_·reh

▶ For travel with children, see page 152.

Complaints

How much longer will our food be?	**C'è ancora molto da aspettare?** cheh ahn·_koh_·rah mohl·toh dah ah·speht·_tah_·reh
We can't wait any longer.	**Non possiamo più aspettare.** nohn pohs·_syah_·moh pyoo ah·speht·_tah_·reh

We're leaving.	**Ce ne andiamo.** cheh neh ahn·<u>dyah</u>·moh
I didn't order this.	**Non è quello che ho ordinato.** nohn eh <u>kwehl</u>·loh keh oh ohr·dee·<u>nah</u>·toh
I ordered…	**Ho ordinato…** oh ohr·dee·<u>nah</u>·toh…
I can't eat this.	**Non lo posso mangiare.** nohn loh <u>pohs</u>·soh mahn·<u>jyah</u>·reh
This is too…	**È troppo…** eh <u>trohp</u>·poh…
– cold/hot	**– freddo/caldo** <u>frehd</u>·doh/<u>kahl</u>·doh
– salty/spicy	**– salato/piccante** sah·<u>lah</u>·toh/peek·<u>kahn</u>·teh
– tough/bland	**– duro/insipido** <u>doo</u>·roh/een·<u>see</u>·pee·doh
This isn't clean/fresh.	**Non è *pulito/fresco.*** nohn eh poo·<u>lee</u>·toh/<u>freh</u>·skoh

Paying

The check [bill], please.	**Il conto, per favore.** eel <u>kohn</u>·toh pehr fah·<u>voh</u>·reh
Separate checks [bills], please.	**Conti separati, per favore.** <u>kohn</u>·tee seh·pah·<u>rah</u>·tee pehr fah·<u>voh</u>·reh
It's all together.	**Conto unico.** <u>kohn</u>·toh <u>oo</u>·nee·koh
Is service included?	**Il servizio è compreso?** eel sehr·<u>vee</u>·tsyoh eh kohm·<u>preh</u>·zoh
What's this amount for?	**Per cos'è questo importo?** pehr koh·<u>zeh</u> <u>kweh</u>·stoh eem·<u>pohr</u>·toh
I didn't have that. I had…	**Questo non è mio. Io ho mangiato…** <u>kweh</u>·stoh nohn eh <u>mee</u>·oh <u>ee</u>·oh oh mahn·<u>jyah</u>·toh…
Can I have *a receipt/ an itemized bill*?	**Posso avere *la fattura/il conto dettagliato*?** <u>pohs</u>·soh ah·<u>veh</u>·reh lah faht·<u>too</u>·rah/ eel <u>kohn</u>·toh eht·tah·<u>llyah</u>·toh
That was delicious!	**Era squisito!** <u>eh</u>·rah skwee·<u>zee</u>·toh

Restaurants charge a **coperto** (service charge) but tipping 10–15% of the bill is common for good service. Tipping is customary in finer restaurants.

Eating Out

Market

Where are the *carts [trolleys]/baskets*?	**Dove sono i *carrelli/cestini*?** doh·veh soh· noh ee *kahr·rehl·lee/cheh·stee·nee*
Where is/Where are…?	**Dov'è/Dove sono…?** doh·veh/doh·veh soh·noh…

▶ For food items, see page 90.

I'd like some of *that/this.*	**Vorrei un po' di *quello/questo.*** vohr·ray oon poh dee *kwehl·loh/kweh·stoh*
Can I taste it?	**Posso assaggiarlo?** pohs·soh ahs·sah·djahr·loh
I'd like…	**Vorrei…** vohr·ray…
– a *kilo/half-kilo* of…	**– un *chilo/mezzo chilo* di…** oon *kee·loh/meh·dzoh kee·loh* dee…
– a liter of…	**– un litro di…** oon lee·troh dee…
– a piece of…	**– un pezzo di…** oon peh·tsoh dee…
– a slice of…	**– una fetta di…** oo·nah feht·tah dee…
More./Less.	**Di più./Di meno.** dee pyoo/dee meh·noh
How much?	**Quant'è?** kwahn·teh
Where do I pay?	**Dove si paga?** doh·veh see pah·gah
A bag, please.	**Una busta, per favore.** oo·nah boos·tah pehr fah·voh·reh
I'm being helped.	**Mi stanno servendo.** mee stahn·noh sehr·vehn·doh

▶ For conversion tables, see page 182.

63

Posso aiutarla? <u>pohs</u>·soh ah·yoo·<u>tahr</u>·lah	Can I help you?
Desidera? deh·<u>zee</u>·deh·rah	What would you like?
Altro? <u>ahl</u>·troh	Anything else?
Sono...euro. <u>soh</u>·noh...<u>eh</u>·oo·roh	That's...euros.

Visit a **panetteria** (bakery) for fresh and tasty bread products; a **gastronomia** (delicatessen) for cold cuts, prepared meals sold by weight and fresh sandwiches; a **pasticceria** (pastry shop) for desserts; a **gelateria** (ice cream parlor) for ice cream specialties or a **bar** or **caffè** (cafe) for a variety of refreshments and small meals, which are cheaper if consumed standing, but more expensive for table service. You can find inexpensive food items at a local **supermercato** (supermarket).

You May See...

CALORIE	calories
SENZA GRASSI	fat free
CONSERVARE IN FRIGO	keep refrigerated
PUÒ CONTENERE TRACCE DI...	may contain traces of...
PUÒ ESSERE COTTO AL MICROONDE	microwaveable
DA CONSUMARE PREFERIBILMENTE ENTRO...	sell by...
ADATTO AI VEGETARIANI	suitable for vegetarians

Dishes, Utensils and Kitchen Tools

blender	**il frullatore** eel frool·lah·<u>toh</u>·reh
bottle opener	**l'apribottiglie** lah·pree·boht·<u>tee</u>·llyeh
bowl	**la coppa** lah <u>kohp</u>·pah
can opener	**l'apriscatole** lah·pree·<u>skah</u>·toh·leh
chopsticks	**i bastoncini cinesi** ee bah·stohn·<u>chee</u>·nee <u>chee</u>·neh·see
colander	**lo scolapasta** loh skoh·lah·<u>pah</u>·stah
corkscrew	**il cavatappi** eel kah·vah·<u>tahp</u>·pee
cup	**la tazza** lah <u>tah</u>·tsah
fork	**la forchetta** lah fohr·<u>keht</u>·tah
frying pan	**la padella** lah pah·<u>dehl</u>·lah
glass	**il bicchiere** eel beek·<u>kyeh</u>·reh
knife	**il coltello** eel kohl·<u>tehl</u>·loh
measuring *cup/ spoon*	**la tazza di misurazione/il misurino** lah <u>tah</u>·tsah dee mee·soo·rah·<u>tsyoh</u>·neh/ eel mee·soo·<u>ree</u>·noh
napkin	**il tovagliolo** eel toh·vah·<u>llyoh</u>·loh
plate	**il piatto** eel <u>pyaht</u>·toh
pot	**la pentola** lah <u>pehn</u>·toh·lah
spatula	**la spatola** lah <u>spah</u>·toh·lah
spoon	**il cucchiaio** eel kook·<u>kyah</u>·yoh

Meals

Breakfast

l'acqua <u>lah</u>·kwah	water
gli affettati llyee ahf·feht·<u>tah</u>·tee	cold cuts [charcuterie]
il burro eel <u>boor</u>·roh	butter
il *caffè/tè...* eel *kahf·<u>feh</u>/teh...*	coffee/tea...
– con il dolcificante kohn eel dohl·chee·fee·<u>kahn</u>·teh	– with artificial sweetener
– al latte ahl <u>laht</u>·teh	– with milk
– con lo zucchero kohn loh <u>dzook</u>·keh·roh	– with sugar
– decaffeinato <u>deh</u>·kahf·feh·ee·<u>nah</u>·toh	– decaf
– nero <u>neh</u>·roh	– black
i cereali ee cheh·reh·<u>ah</u>·lee	cereal
la farina d'avena lah fah·<u>ree</u>·nah dah·<u>veh</u>·nah	oatmeal
il formaggio eel fohr·<u>mah</u>·djoh	cheese
la frittata lah freet·<u>tah</u>·tah	omelet
il latte eel <u>laht</u>·teh	milk
la marmellata lah mahr·mehl·<u>lah</u>·tah	jam
il muesli eel <u>mweh</u>·slee	granola [muesli]
il muffin eel <u>mahf</u>·feen	muffin
la pancetta lah pahn·<u>cheht</u>·tah	bacon
il pane eel <u>pah</u>·neh	bread
il pane tostato eel <u>pah</u>·neh toh·<u>stah</u>·toh	toast

I'd like...	**Vorrei...** vohr·<u>ray</u>...
More...	**Dell'*altro♂/altra♀*...** dehl·<u>lahl</u>·troh/<u>lahl</u>·trah...

il panino eel pah·nee·noh	roll
la salsiccia lah sahl·see·chyah	sausage
il succo... eel sook·koh...	...juice
– d'arancia dah·rahn·chyah	– orange
– di mela dee meh·lah	– apple
– di pompelmo dee pohm·pehl·moh	– grapefruit
l'uovo... lwoh·voh...	...egg
– fritto freet·toh	– fried
– sodo/alla coque soh·doh/ahl·lah kohk	– hard-/soft-boiled
– strapazzato strah·pah·tsah·toh	– scrambled
lo yogurt loh yoh·goort	yogurt

Appetizers [Starters]

l'acciuga lah·chyoo·ghah	anchovy
l'affettato lahf·feht·tah·toh	platter of cold cuts
le alici a scapece leh ah·lee·chee ah skah·peh·cheh	fresh fried anchovies marinated in vinegar and spices
l'antipasto misto lahn·tee·pah·stoh mee·stoh	assorted appetizers
la bresaola lah breh·sah·oh·lah	cured raw beef
i carciofini sott'olio ee kar·chyoh·fee·nee soht·toh·lyoh	artichoke hearts in olive oil
la coppa lah kohp·pah	cured pork shoulder
i crostini ee kroh·stee·nee	toast topped with a variety of ingredients, including tomatoes, sardines and cheese

| With/Without... | **Con/Senza...** kohn/sehn·tsah... |
| I can't have... | **Non posso mangiare...** nohn pohs·soh mahn·jyah·reh... |

la caprese lah kah·*preh*·seh	sliced tomatoes, mozzarella and basil dressed with olive oil
l'insalata di frutti di mare leen·sah·*lah*·tah dee *froot*·tee dee *mah*·reh	seafood salad
la mortadella lah mohr·tah·*dehl*·lah	Bologna sausage
la peperonata lah peh·peh·roh·*nah*·tah	mixed sweet peppers stewed with tomatoes
il prosciutto crudo di Parma eel proh·*shyoot*·toh *kroo*·doh dee *pahr*·mah	cured ham from Parma
i sottaceti ee soht·tah·*cheh*·tee	pickled vegetables

Soup

l'acquacotta lah·kwah·*koht*·tah	Tuscan vegetable soup with poached egg
il brodo di manzo eel *broh*·doh dee *mahn*·dzoh	beef broth
il brodo di pollo eel *broh*·doh dee *pohl*·loh	chicken broth
la buridda lah boo·*reed*·dah	fish stew
il cacciucco eel kah·*chyook*·koh	spicy seafood chowder
il cacciucco alla livornese eel kah·*chyook*·koh *ahl*·lah lee·vohr·*neh*·seh	tomato seafood chowder
la crema di legumi lah *kreh*·mah dee leh·*goo*·mee	vegetable cream soup
il minestrone eel mee·neh·*stroh*·neh	mixed vegetable and bean soup
la ribollita lah ree·bohl·*lee*·tah	Tuscan bean, vegetable and bread soup

I'd like…	**Vorrei…** vohr·*ray*…
More…	**Dell'*altro*♂/*altra*♀…** dehl·*lah*·troh/*lah*·trah…

lo spezzatino loh speh·tsah·<u>tee</u>·noh	meat stew
la zuppa di fagioli lah <u>dzoop</u>·pah dee fah·<u>jyoh</u>·lee	bean soup
la zuppa alla pavese lah <u>dzoop</u>·pah <u>ahl</u>·lah pah·<u>veh</u>·seh	consommé with poached egg, croutons and grated cheese
la zuppa di pollo lah <u>dzoop</u>·pah dee <u>pohl</u>·loh	chicken soup
la zuppa di pomodoro lah <u>dzoop</u>·pah dee poh·moh·<u>doh</u>·roh	tomato soup
la zuppa di verdure lah <u>dzoop</u>·pah dee vehr·<u>doo</u>·reh	vegetable soup
la zuppa di vongole lah <u>dzoop</u>·pah dee <u>vohn</u>·goh·leh	clam and white wine soup

Fish and Seafood

l'acciuga lah·<u>chyoo</u>·ghah	anchovy
l'anguilla lahn·<u>gweel</u>·lah	eel
l'anguilla alla veneziana lahn·<u>gweel</u>·lah <u>ahl</u>·lah veh·neh·<u>tsyah</u>·nah	eel cooked in tomato sauce, a specialty of Venice
l'aragosta lah·rah·<u>goh</u>·stah	lobster
l'aringa lah·<u>reen</u>·gah	herring
il baccalà eel bahk·kah·<u>lah</u>	salted, dried cod
il branzino eel brahn·<u>dzee</u>·noh	sea bass
i calamari ee kah·lah·<u>mah</u>·ree	squid
le cozze leh <u>koh</u>·tseh	mussels
le cozze ripiene leh <u>koh</u>·tseh ree·<u>pyeh</u>·neh	stuffed mussels

With/Without…	**Con/Senza…** kohn/<u>sehn</u>·tsah…
I can't have…	**Non posso mangiare…** nohn <u>pohs</u>·soh mahn·<u>jyah</u>·reh…

69

il fritto misto eel <u>freet</u>·toh <u>mee</u>·stoh	mixed fried fish with shellfish
i gamberi ee <u>gahm</u>·beh·ree	shrimp
i gamberi grigliati ee <u>gahm</u>·beh·ree gree·<u>llyah</u>·tee	grilled shrimp with garlic
il granchio eel <u>grahn</u>·kyoh	crab
le lumache leh loo·<u>mah</u>·keh	snails
le lumache alla milanese leh loo·<u>mah</u>·keh <u>ahl</u>·lah mee·lah·<u>neh</u>·seh	snails with anchovy, fennel and wine sauce
il merluzzo eel mehr·<u>loo</u>·tsoh	cod
la moleca lah moh·<u>leh</u>·kah	soft shell crab
l'orata loh·<u>rah</u>·tah	sea bream
le ostriche leh <u>oh</u>·stree·keh	oysters
il pesce spada eel <u>peh</u>·sheh <u>spah</u>·dah	swordfish
il polpo eel <u>pohl</u>·poh	octopus
il salmone eel sahl·<u>moh</u>·neh	salmon
la sardina lah sahr·<u>dee</u>·nah	sardine
lo scorfano loh <u>skohr</u>·fah·noh	hog fish
la sogliola lah <u>soh</u>·llyoh·lah	sole
lo stoccafisso loh stohk·kah·<u>fees</u>·soh	dried cod cooked with tomatoes, olives and artichoke
il tonno eel <u>tohn</u>·noh	tuna
la trota lah <u>troh</u>·tah	trout
le vongole leh <u>vohn</u>·goh·leh	clams

I'd like…	**Vorrei…** vohr·<u>ray</u>…
More…	**Dell'*altro*♂ /*altra*♀ …** dehl·<u>lahl</u>·troh/<u>lahl</u>·trah…

Meat and Poultry

l'abbacchio alla romana lahb·<u>bahk</u>·kyoh ahl·lah roh·<u>mah</u>·nah
roasted spring lamb, a specialty of Rome

l'agnello lah·<u>nyehl</u>·loh
lamb

l'anatra <u>lah</u>·nah·trah
duck

la bistecca lah bee·<u>stehk</u>·kah
steak

la bistecca alla fiorentina lah bee·<u>stehk</u>·kah ahl·lah fyoh·rehn·<u>tee</u>·nah
grilled T-bone steak, a specialty of Florence

la braciola lah brah·<u>chyoh</u>·lah
grilled pork chop

il capretto eel kah·<u>preht</u>·toh
goat

la cima alla genovese lah <u>chee</u>·mah ahl·lah jeh·noh·<u>veh</u>·seh
flank steak stuffed with eggs and vegetables, a specialty of Genoa

il cinghiale eel cheen·<u>ghyah</u>·leh
wild boar, usually braised or roasted

il coniglio eel koh·<u>nee</u>·llyoh
rabbit

la cotoletta alla milanese lah koh·toh·<u>leht</u>·tah ahl·lah mee·lah·<u>neh</u>·seh
breaded veal cutlet flavored with cheese

la cotoletta di vitello con fontina lah koh·toh·<u>leht</u>·tah dee vee·<u>tehl</u>·loh kohn fohn·<u>tee</u>·nah
veal cutlet stuffed with fontina cheese, breaded and sautéed

il fagiano eel fah·<u>jyah</u>·noh
pheasant

il fegato eel <u>feh</u>·gah·toh
liver

il fegato alla veneziana eel <u>feh</u>·gah·toh ahl·lah veh·neh·<u>tsyah</u>·nah
thin slices of calf's liver fried with onions

il filetto al pepe verde eel fee·<u>leht</u>·toh ahl <u>peh</u>·peh <u>vehr</u>·deh
filet steak in a creamy sauce with green peppercorns

With/Without...	**Con/Senza...** kohn/<u>sehn</u>·tsah...
I can't have...	**Non posso mangiare...** nohn <u>pohs</u>·soh mahn·<u>jyah</u>·reh...

gli involtini llyee een·vohl·tee·nee	thin slices of meat rolled and stuffed
la luganega lah loo·gah·neh·gah	type of pork sausage
il maiale eel mah·yah·leh	pork
il manzo eel mahn·dzoh	beef
il montone eel mohn·toh·neh	mutton
l'oca loh·kah	goose
l'osso buco lohs·soh boo·koh	braised veal shank
la pancetta lah pahn·cheht·tah	bacon
la piccata al Marsala lah peek·kah·tah ahl mahr·sah·lah	thin cutlets cooked in Marsala sauce
il pollo eel pohl·loh	chicken
il pollo alla cacciatora eel pohl·loh ahl·lah kah·chyah·toh·rah	chicken braised with mushrooms in tomato sauce
il pollo alla diavola eel pohl·loh ahl·lah dyah·voh·lah	chicken grilled with lemon and hot pepper
il pollo al mattone eel pohl·loh ahl maht·toh·neh	chicken cooked with herbs in a brick oven
il pollo alla romana eel pohl·loh ahl·lah roh·mah·nah	diced chicken with tomato sauce and sweet peppers

rare	**al sangue** ahl sahn·gweh
medium	**mediamente cotta** meh·dyah·mehn·teh koht·tah
well-done	**ben cotta** behn koht·tah

I'd like…	**Vorrei…** vohr·ray…
More…	**Dell'*altro*♂ /*altra*♀ …** dehl·lah·troh/lah·trah…

la polpetta lah pohl·<u>peht</u>·tah	meatball
la porchetta lah pohr·<u>keht</u>·tah	suckling pig
il prosciutto eel proh·<u>shyoot</u>·toh	ham
la quaglia lah <u>kwah</u>·llyah	quail
la salsiccia lah sahl·<u>see</u>·chyah	sausage
il saltimbocca eel sahl·teem·<u>bohk</u>·kah	veal and ham roll
il tacchino eel tahk·<u>kee</u>·noh	turkey
il vitello eel vee·<u>tehl</u>·loh	veal

In Italy, pizza is generally served in a size suitable for one person, though it can be shared. Pizza is usually thin crusted, about the size of a dinner plate, and is eaten with a knife and fork. Some pizzerias, though, may ask if you want your pizza **sottile** (thin) or **alta** (literally, high; here it means thick). There are many varieties of pizza and most are topped with mozzarella cheese; listed below are some of the most popular.

Pizza

la pizza... lah <u>pee</u>·tsah...	...pizza
– **bianca** <u>byahn</u>·kah	– "white," without tomato sauce
– **con i funghi** kohn ee <u>foon</u>·ghee	– with mushrooms
– **dolce** <u>dohl</u>·cheh	– with a variety of sweet toppings, served as a dessert

With/Without...	**Con/Senza...** kohn/<u>sehn</u>·tsah...	
I can't have...	**Non posso mangiare...** nohn <u>pohs</u>·soh mahn·<u>jyah</u>·reh...	

– **margherita** mahr·gheh·<u>ree</u>·tah	– tomato, cheese and basil or oregano, named after Italy's first queen and reflecting the national colors
– **marinara** mah·ree·<u>nah</u>·rah	– with tomato sauce, garlic, capers, oregano and sometimes anchovies
– **napoletana** nah·poh·leh·<u>tah</u>·nah	– anchovies, tomatoes, cheese and sometimes capers
– **quattro formaggi** <u>kwaht</u>·troh fohr·<u>mah</u>·djee	– with four types of cheese
– **quattro stagioni** <u>kwaht</u>·troh stah·<u>jyoh</u>·nee	– "four seasons", with tomatoes, artichokes, mushrooms, olives; plus cheese, ham and bacon
– **rustica** roos·tee·kah	– with ricotta, mozzarella, prosciutto, mortadella and seasonings

| I'd like… | **Vorrei…** vohr·<u>ray</u>… |
| More… | **Dell'_altro_♂ /_altra_♀ …** dehl·<u>lah</u>l·troh/<u>lah</u>l·trah… |

ROMANA
ITALIA

TONNO OLIVE

CAPRICCIOSA

QUATTRO STAGIONI   MIX

FUNGHI

TOMATO · CHEESE · FRESH TOMATO BASIL
TOMATEN · KÄSE · FRISCHE TOMATEN · BASILIKUM
TOMATO · FROMAGE · TOMATO FRAIS · BASILIC
TOMATO · QUESO · LONGHAS DE TOMATE FRESCO · ALBAHACA
TOMATE · QUEIJO · TALHADA DE TOMATE FRESCO · BASILICAO

TOMATO · QUESO · ANCHOA
TOMATO · FROMAGE · ANCHOIS

TOMATO · CHEESE · TUNAFISH · O
TOMATEN · KÄSE · THUNFISH · OLI
TOMATO · FROMAGE · THONFISCH ·
TOMATO · QUESO · ATUN · ACEIT
TOMATE · QUEIJO · ATUM · AZEI

TOMATO · CHEESE · HAM · MUSHROOM
TOMATEN · KÄSE · SCHINKEN · PIL
TOMATO · FROMAGE · JAMBON · CHAM
TOMATO · QUEIJO · JAMON · HONG
TOMATO · QUESO · PRESUNTO · COG

TOMATO · CHEESE · MUSHROOMS
TOMATEN · KÄSE · PILZ
TOMATO · FROMAGE · CHAMPIGNON

NO SER
NO COVE

Pasta

gli agnolotti llyee ah·nyoh·<u>loht</u>·tee | meat-stuffed pasta

i cannelloni ee kahn·nehl·<u>loh</u>·nee | stuffed pasta tubes, topped with sauce

i cappelletti ee kahp·pehl·<u>leht</u>·tee | small ravioli filled with meat, ham, cheese and eggs

i capelli d'angelo ee kah·<u>pehl</u>·lee dahn·<u>jeh</u>·loh | angelhair pasta

le fettuccine leh feht·too·<u>chee</u>·neh | broad, long pasta made from eggs and flour

i fusilli ee foo·<u>seel</u>·lee | spiral-shaped pasta

gli gnocchi llyee <u>nyohk</u>·kee | small potato dumplings

With/Without… | **Con/Senza…** kohn/<u>sehn</u>·tsah…
I can't have… | **Non posso mangiare…** nohn <u>pohs</u>·soh mahn·<u>jyah</u>·reh…

le lasagne leh lah·<u>sah</u>·nyeh	thin pasta strips layered with tomato or white sauce, meat and cheese
le linguine leh leen·<u>gwee</u>·neh	narrow, long pasta
le orecchiette leh oh·reh·<u>kyeht</u>·teh	small, shell-shaped pasta
i pansotti ee pahn·<u>soht</u>·tee	swiss chard- and herb-stuffed pasta, usually served with a walnut sauce
le pappardelle leh pahp·pahr·<u>dehl</u>·leh	long, rectangular pasta of medium width with ribbon edges
la pastina lah pahs·<u>tee</u>·nah	tiny, dried pasta used in soups
le penne leh <u>pehn</u>·neh	short, tubular pasta with angled ends
i quadrucci ee kwah·<u>droo</u>·chee	stuffed pasta squares added to soup
i rigatoni ee ree·gah·<u>toh</u>·nee	fat tubes of dried pasta with ridges
gli spaghetti llyee spah·<u>gheht</u>·tee	long thin strands of fresh pasta
le tagliatelle leh tah·llyah·<u>tehl</u>·leh	thin, long pasta with ribbon edges
i tortelli ee tohr·<u>tehl</u>·lee	stuffed rectangular or square fresh pasta

I'd like…	**Vorrei…** vohr·<u>ray</u>…
More…	**Dell'altro**♂ **/ altra**♀ **…** dehl·<u>lahl</u>·troh/<u>lahl</u>·trah…

i tortellini ee tohr·tehl·<u>lee</u>·nee	small stuffed pasta nuggets
gli ziti llyee <u>tsee</u>·tee	tubular pasta

Pasta Sauces ─────────────

all'agliata ahl·lah·<u>llyah</u>·tah	hot and spicy sauce with garlic
all'Alfredo ahl·lahl·<u>freh</u>·doh	butter and parmesan cheese
all'amatriciana ahl·lah·mah·tree·<u>chyah</u>·nah	bacon and tomato
alla bolognese <u>ahl</u>·lah boh·loh·<u>nyeh</u>·seh	ground meat and tomato
alla boscaiola <u>ahl</u>·lah boh·skah·<u>yoh</u>·lah	tomatoes, butter, cheese, mushrooms, olive oil and garlic
alla carbonara <u>ahl</u>·lah kahr·boh·<u>nah</u>·rah	bacon and egg
fra' diavolo frah <u>dyah</u>·voh·loh	tomato with hot pepper
alla marinara <u>ahl</u>·lah mah·ree·<u>nah</u>·rah	tomato, olive oil and garlic
alla napoletana <u>ahl</u>·lah nah·poh·leh·<u>tah</u>·nah	cheese, tomatoes and herbs
al pesto ahl <u>peh</u>·stoh	ground basil, garlic, parmesan and pine nuts
al pomodoro ahl poh·moh·<u>doh</u>·roh	simple tomato sauce
alla puttanesca <u>ahl</u>·lah poot·tah·<u>neh</u>·skah	tomatoes, black olives, peppers, olive oil and garlic

With/Without…	**Con/Senza…** kohn/<u>sehn</u>·tsah…
I can't have…	**Non posso mangiare…** nohn <u>pohs</u>·soh mahn·<u>jyah</u>·reh…

al ragù ahl rah·<u>goo</u> — with meat

alla siciliana <u>ahl</u>·lah see·chee·<u>lyah</u>·nah — provolone and eggplant

alle vongole <u>ahl</u>·leh vohn·goh·leh — clams and tomato

Vegetables and Staples

l'aceto lah·<u>cheh</u>·toh — vinegar

l'aglio <u>lah</u>·llyoh — garlic

l'asparago lah·<u>spah</u>·rah·goh — asparagus

l'avocado lah·voh·<u>kah</u>·doh — avocado

la barbabietola lah bahr·bah·<u>byeh</u>·toh·lah — beet

la bietola lah <u>byeh</u>·toh·lah — swiss chard

i broccoli ee <u>brohk</u>·koh·lee — broccoli

il carciofo eel kahr·<u>chyoh</u>·foh — artichoke

i carciofi alla guidea ee kahr·<u>chyoh</u>·fee <u>ahl</u>·lah gwee·<u>deh</u>·ah — crispy deep-fried artichokes, originally a specialty of the Jewish quarter in Rome

i carciofi alla romana ee kahr·<u>chyoh</u>·fee <u>ahl</u>·lah roh·<u>mah</u>·nah — whole lightly stewed artichokes stuffed with garlic, salt, olive oil, wild mint and parsley

la carota lah kah·<u>roh</u>·tah — carrot

il cavolfiore eel kah·vohl·<u>fyoh</u>·reh — cauliflower

il cavolo eel <u>kah</u>·voh·loh — cabbage

i ceci ee <u>cheh</u>·chee — chickpeas

il cetriolo eel cheh·<u>tryoh</u>·loh — cucumber

la cipolla lah chee·<u>pohl</u>·lah — onion

I'd like… **Vorrei…** vohr·<u>ray</u>…

More… **Dell'*altro*♂ / *altra*♀ …** dehl·<u>lahl</u>·troh/<u>lahl</u>·trah…

i fagioli ee fah·<u>jyoh</u>·lee	beans
i fagioli alla toscana ee fah·<u>jyoh</u>·lee <u>ahl</u>·lah toh·<u>skah</u>·nah	Tuscan-style beans seasoned with salt, black pepper and olive oil
i fagioli in umido ee fah·<u>jyoh</u>·lee een <u>oo</u>·mee·doh	beans cooked in tomato sauce and spices
i fagiolini ee fah·jyoh·<u>lee</u>·nee	green beans
le fave leh <u>fah</u>·veh	broad beans
i funghi ee <u>foon</u>·ghee	mushrooms
i funghi porcini arrostiti ee <u>foon</u>·ghee pohr·<u>chee</u>·nee ahr·roh·<u>stee</u>·tee	porcini mushrooms roasted or grilled with garlic, parsley and chili peppers
la lattuga lah laht·<u>too</u>·gah	lettuce
il mais eel <u>mah</u>·ees	corn
la melanzana lah meh·lahn·<u>tsah</u>·nah	eggplant [aubergine]
l'oliva loh·<u>lee</u>·vah	olive
l'ortaggio lohr·<u>tah</u>·djoh	vegetable
la pasta lah <u>pah</u>·stah	pasta
la patata lah pah·<u>tah</u>·tah	potato
il pepe *bianco/nero* eel <u>peh</u>·peh <u>byahn</u>·koh/<u>neh</u>·roh	*white/black* pepper
il pepe rosso eel <u>peh</u>·peh <u>rohs</u>·soh	paprika
il peperone *rosso/verde* eel peh·peh·<u>roh</u>·neh <u>rohs</u>·soh/<u>vehr</u>·deh	*red/green* pepper
i piselli ee pee·<u>tsehl</u>·lee	peas

With/Without…	**Con/Senza…** kohn/<u>sehn</u>·tsah…
I can't have…	**Non posso mangiare…** nohn <u>pohs</u>·soh mahn·<u>jyah</u>·reh…

i piselli al prosciutto ee pee·<u>tsehl</u>·lee ahl proh·<u>shyoot</u>·toh	peas with ham
la polenta lah poh·<u>lehn</u>·tah	cornmeal
la polenta al nero di seppia lah poh·<u>lehn</u>·tah ahl <u>neh</u>·roh dee <u>sehp</u>·pyah	polenta with baby squid in its own ink
il pomodoro eel poh·moh·<u>doh</u>·roh	tomato
i porri con le patate ee <u>pohr</u>·ree kohn leh pah·<u>tah</u>·teh	leek and potato casserole
il riso eel <u>ree</u>·zoh	rice
il risotto eel ree·<u>zoh</u>·toh	arborio rice cooked slowly in broth, with seafood, vegetables, etc.
il sale eel <u>sah</u>·leh	salt
il sedano eel seh·<u>dah</u>·noh	celery
gli spinaci llyee spee·<u>nah</u>·chee	spinach
lo zucchero loh <u>tsook</u>·keh·roh	sugar
la zucchina lah tsook·<u>kee</u>·nah	zucchini [courgette]

Fruit

l'ananas <u>lah</u>·nah·nahs	pineapple
l'anguria lahn·<u>goo</u>·ryah	watermelon (northern Italy)
l'albicocca lahl·bee·<u>kohk</u>·kah	apricot
l'arancia lah·<u>rahn</u>·chah	orange
la banana lah bah·<u>nah</u>·nah	banana
il cedro eel <u>cheh</u>·droh	lime

I'd like…	**Vorrei…** vohr·<u>ray</u>…
More…	**Dell'altro**♂ **/altra**♀ **…** dehl·<u>lahl</u>·troh/<u>lahl</u>·trah…

la ciliegia lah chee·<u>lyeh</u>·jyah	cherry
il cocomero eel koh·<u>koh</u>·meh·roh	watermelon (Rome & southern Italy)
la fragola lah <u>frah</u>·goh·lah	strawberry
la frutta lah <u>froot</u>·tah	fruit
il lampone eel lahm·<u>poh</u>·neh	raspberry
il limone eel lee·<u>moh</u>·neh	lemon
la mela lah <u>meh</u>·lah	apple
il melone eel meh·<u>loh</u>·neh	melon
il mirtillo eel meer·<u>teel</u>·loh	blueberry
la pera lah <u>peh</u>·rah	pear
la pesca lah <u>peh</u>·skah	peach
il pompelmo eel pohm·<u>pehl</u>·moh	grapefruit
la prugna lah <u>proo</u>·nyah	plum
l'uva <u>loo</u>·vah	grape

Cheese

il formaggio… eel fohr·<u>mah</u>·djoh…	…cheese
– asiago ah·<u>syah</u>·goh	– nutty-flavored
– Bel Paese behl pah·<u>eh</u>·seh	– smooth and delicate
– bocconcini bohk·kohn·<u>chee</u>·nee	– small balls of fresh mozzarella
– caciocavallo kah·chyoh·kah·<u>vahl</u>·loh	– firm, slightly sweet, made with cow's or sheep's milk
– caciotta kah·<u>chyoht</u>·tah	– firm, usually mild

With/Without…	**Con/Senza…** kohn/<u>sehn</u>·tsah…
I can't have…	**Non posso mangiare…** nohn <u>pohs</u>·soh mahn·<u>jyah</u>·reh…

– **caprino** kah·<u>pree</u>·noh	– made from goat's milk
– **crescenza** kreh·<u>shehn</u>·tsah	– rich and creamy
– **dolce** <u>dohl</u>·cheh	– mild
– **dolcelatte** dohl·cheh·<u>laht</u>·teh	– mild, creamy, blue-veined
– **duro** <u>doo</u>·roh	– hard
– **fontina** fohn·<u>tee</u>·nah	– full-fat and semi-hard
– **gorgonzola** gohr·gohn·<u>dzoh</u>·lah	– strong and blue-veined
– **grana** <u>grah</u>·nah	– similar to parmesan
– **gruviera** groo·<u>vyeh</u>·rah	– sweet, nutlike flavor, similar to Swiss gruyere
– **mascarpone** mahs·kahr·<u>poh</u>·neh	– used like whipped cream
– **molle** <u>mohl</u>·leh	– soft
– **mozzarella** moh·tsah·<u>rehl</u>·lah	– full-fat and mild, made with cow's or buffalo's milk
– **parmigiano** pahr·mee·<u>jyah</u>·noh	– parmesan
– **pecorino** peh·koh·<u>ree</u>·noh	– strong, made with sheep's milk
– **piccante** peek·<u>kahn</u>·teh	– sharp
– **provolone** proh·voh·<u>loh</u>·neh	– firm and flavorful
– **ricotta** ree·<u>koht</u>·tah	– soft and mild, made with cow's or sheep's milk

I'd like…	**Vorrei…** vohr·<u>ray</u>…
More…	**Dell'*altro*♂/*altra*♀ …** dehl·<u>lahl</u>·troh/<u>lahl</u>·trah…

Dessert

gli amaretti llyee ah·mah·<u>reht</u>·tee	almond cookies
il biscotto eel bees·<u>koht</u>·toh	crunchy cookie for dipping into coffee or wine
il budino eel boo·<u>dee</u>·noh	pudding
i cannoli ee kahn·<u>noh</u>·lee	crispy pastry tubes filled with sweetened ricotta and candied fruit
la cassata siciliana lah kahs·<u>sah</u>·tah see·chee·<u>lyah</u>·nah	traditional Sicilian cake with ricotta, chocolate and candied fruit
il castagnaccio eel kah·stah·<u>nyah</u>·chyoh	deep-fried chestnut cake
la crema lah <u>kreh</u>·mah	custard

With/Without...	**Con/Senza...** kohn/<u>sehn</u>·tsah...
I can't have...	**Non posso mangiare...** nohn <u>pohs</u>·soh mahn·<u>jyah</u>·reh...

la crostata lah kroh·<u>stah</u>·tah	pie
i dolci ee <u>dohl</u>·chee	sweets
il gelato eel jeh·<u>lah</u>·toh	ice cream
i gianduiotti ee jyahn·<u>dyoht</u>·tee	chocolate drops from Turin
la granita lah grah·<u>nee</u>·tah	frozen fruit-juice slush
il pandolce eel pahn·<u>dohl</u>·cheh	yeast cake with grapes and raisins
il panettone eel pah·neht·<u>toh</u>·neh	Christmas sweet bread with raisins and candied citrus peel
il panforte eel pahn·<u>fohr</u>·teh	dense cake made of almond, candied citrus, spices and honey
la panna cotta lah <u>pahn</u>·nah <u>koht</u>·tah	molded chilled cream pudding
il tartufo eel tahr·<u>too</u>·foh	chocolate truffle dessert
il tiramisù eel tee·rah·mee·<u>soo</u>	coffee- and rum-flavored layered dessert
la torta lah <u>tohr</u>·tah	cake
lo zabaglione loh dzah·bah·<u>llyoh</u>·neh	warm custard with Marsala wine
lo zuccotto loh dzook·<u>koht</u>·toh	sponge cake filled with fresh cream, chocolate, candied fruit and liqueur

I'd like…	**Vorrei…** vohr·<u>ray</u>…
More…	**Dell'altro♂ /altra♀…** dehl·<u>lahl</u>·troh/<u>lahl</u>·trah…
With/Without…	**Con/Senza…** kohn/<u>sehn</u>·tsah…
I can't have…	**Non posso mangiare…** nohn <u>pohs</u>·soh mahn·<u>jyah</u>·reh…

84

i The Italian **gelato**, similar to ice cream, is made from milk and sugar—not cream. Though it has less fat content than ice cream, it is still very dense and creamy. Popular flavors include **caffè** (coffee), **cioccolato** (chocolate), **fragola** (strawberry), **frutti di bosco** (mixed berries), **gianduia** (chocolate hazelnut), **limone** (lemon), **nocciola** (hazelnut), **pistacchio** (pistachio) and **vaniglia** (vanilla).

Drinks

Essential

The *wine/drink* menu, please.	**La *carta dei vini/lista delle bevande*, per favore.** lah _kahr_·tah day _vee_·nee/_lee_·stah _dehl_·leh beh·_vahn_·deh pehr fah·_voh_·reh
What do you recommend?	**Cosa mi consiglia?** _koh_·zah mee kohn·_see_·llyah
I'd like *a bottle/ glass* of *red/ white* wine.	**Vorrei *una bottiglia/un bicchiere* di vino *rosso/bianco*.** vohr·_ray_ _oo_·nah boht·_tee_·llyah/ oon beek·_kyeh_·reh dee _vee_·noh _rohs_·soh/ _byahn_·koh
The house wine, please.	**Il vino della casa, per favore.** eel _vee_·noh _dehl_·lah _kah_·zah pehr fah·_voh_·reh
Another *bottle/ glass,* please.	**Un'altra bottiglia/Un altro bicchiere, per favore.** oo·_nahl_·trah boht·_tee_·llyah/oo·_nahl_·troh beek·_kyeh_·reh pehr fah·_voh_·reh
I'd like a local beer.	**Vorrei una birra locale.** vohr·_ray_ _oo_·nah _beer_·rah loh·_kah_·leh
Can I buy you a drink?	**Posso offrirle qualcosa?** _pohs_·soh ohf·_freer_·leh kwahl·_koh_·sah
Cheers!	**Salute!** sah·_loo_·teh

A *coffee/tea*, please.	**Un *caffè/tè*, per favore.** oon *kahf-feh/teh* pehr fah-voh-reh
Black.	**Nero.** neh-roh
With…	**Con…** kohn…
– some milk	**– un po' di latte** oon poh dee laht-teh
– sugar	**– lo zucchero** loh dzook-keh-roh
– artificial sweetener	**– il dolcificante** eel dohl-chee-fee-kahn-teh
…, please.	**…, per favore.** …pehr fah-voh-reh
– A juice	**– Un succo** oon sook-koh
– A soda	**– Una bibita** oo-nah bee-bee-tah
– A (sparkling/still) water	**– Un bicchiere d'acqua (frizzante/naturale)** oon beek-kyeh-reh dah-kwah (free-dzahn-teh/nah-too-rah-leh)

Non-alcoholic Drinks

l'acqua (frizzante/naturale) lah-kwah (free-dzahn-teh/nah-too-rah-leh)	(sparkling/still) water
la bibita lah bee-bee-tah	soda
il caffè eel kahf-feh	coffee
il latte eel laht-teh	milk
la limonata lah lee-moh-nah-tah	lemon soda
il succo eel sook-koh	juice
il tè (freddo) eel teh (frehd-doh)	(iced) tea
la spremuta lah spreh-moo-tah	fresh-squeezed fruit juice

i **Il caffè** (coffee) has been a very popular drink in Italy since the 16th century, when the first European coffeehouse opened in Venice. Italians usually stop to drink a coffee—standing at the bar—on their way to work. If you have time to spare, you may wish to sit and enjoy your beverage, but you'll pay extra for table service. It is customary to have a cup of coffee after your meal. Popular types of Italian coffee include:

caffè: strong coffee, similar to espresso elsewhere
doppio: double serving of **caffè**
ristretto: very strong coffee, made with less water
americano: weak coffee, made with more water
macchiato: coffee served with steamed milk
cappuccino: equal parts coffee, steamed milk and milk foam

Posso offrirle qualcosa?
pohs·soh ohf·freer·leh kwahl·koh·zah

Can I get you a drink?

Con latte o zucchero?
kohn laht·teh oh dzook·keh·roh

With milk or sugar?

Acqua frizzante o naturale?
ah·kwah free·dzahn·teh
oh nah·too·rah·leh

Sparkling or still
water?

Aperitifs, Cocktails and Liqueurs

l'amaretto lah·mah·reht·toh	almond liqueur
l'amaro lah·mah·roh	bitter
il brandy eel brahn·dee	brandy
il digestivo eel dee·jehs·tee·voh	after-dinner drink
il gin eel jeen	gin
il rum eel room	rum
la sambuca lah sahm·boo·kah	aniseed-flavored liqueur
lo scotch loh skohtch	scotch
la strega lah streh·gah	sweet herb liqueur
la tequila la teh·kee·lah	tequila
la vodka la vohd·kah	vodka
il whisky eel whees·kee	whisky

Beer

la birra... lah beer·rah... ...beer

– in bottiglia/alla spina een
boht·tee·llyah/ahl·lah spee·nah

– bottled/draft

– scura/chiara skoo·rah/kyah·rah – dark/light

- **lager/pilsner** <u>lah</u>·gehr/<u>peels</u>·nehr
- **nazionale/importata** nah·tsyoh·<u>nah</u>·leh/
  eem·pohr·<u>tah</u>·tah
- **analcolica** ah·nahl·<u>koh</u>·lee·kah

– lager/pilsner	
– local/imported	
– non-alcoholic	

Wine

lo champagne loh shahm·<u>pah</u>·nyeh — champagne

il vino... eel <u>vee</u>·noh... — ...wine

- **rosso/bianco** <u>rohs</u>·soh/<u>byahn</u>·koh — red/white
- **della casa/da tavola** <u>dehl</u>·lah <u>kah</u>·zah/dah <u>tah</u>·voh·lah — house/table
- **secco/dolce** <u>sehk</u>·koh/<u>dohl</u>·cheh — dry/sweet
- **frizzante** free·<u>dzahn</u>·teh — sparkling
- **da dessert** dah dehs·<u>sehrt</u> — dessert

---

i Popular types of Italian wine are listed below. The region where the wine is typically found is listed in parentheses.

sparkling sweet wine	Asti spumante (Piedmont); Prosecco (Veneto)
red wine	Nebbiolo (Piedmont); Amarone, Valpolicella (Veneto); Brunello di Montalcino, Chianti, Sangiovese (Tuscany); Corvo Rosso, Nero d'Avola (Sicily)
rosé	Lagrein (Trentino-Alto Adige)
dry white wine	Frascati (Latium); Orvieto (Umbria); Pinot grigio (Veneto); Vermentino (Sardinia)
dessert wine	Vin santo (Tuscany)

MARGHERITA

TOMATO CHEESE
TOMATEN KÄSE
TOMATO FROMAGE
TOMATO QUEIJO
PRESUNTO QUEIJO

PROSCIUTTO

TOMATO · CHEESE · HAM
TOMATO · QUESO · JAMON
TOMATEN · KÄSE · SCHINKEN
TOMATO · FROMAGE · JAMBON
TOMATE · QUEIJO · PRESUNTO

DIAVOLA

TOMATO CHEESE PEPPERONI
TOMATEN · KÄSE · SALAMI
TOMATO · FROMAGE SAUCISSON
TOMATO · QUESO · CHORIZO
TOMATE · QUEIJO · PAIO

VERDURE

TOMATO · CHEESE · PEPPER · EGGPLANT COURG
TOMATEN · KÄSE · PAPRIKA · AUBERGINE · COURGET
TOMATO · FROMAGE · POIVRON · AUBERGINE · COURGE
TOMATO · QUESO · PIMENTON · BERENJENA · CALABAC
TOMATE · QUEIJO · PIMENTAO · BERENJENA · ABOBRI

PUGLIESE

TOMATO · CHEESE · OLIVE
TOMATEN · KÄSE · OLIVES
TOMATO · FROMAGE OLIVE
TOMATO QUESO ACEITUNA
TOMATE · QUEIJO · AZEITONA

l'abbacchio lahb·bahk·kyoh	lamb
l'acciuga lah·chyoo·ghah	anchovy
l'aceto lah·cheh·toh	vinegar
l'aceto balsamico lah·cheh·toh bahl·sah·mee·koh	balsamic vinegar
l'acqua lah·kwah	water
l'acqua tonica lah·kwah toh·nee·kah	tonic water
gli affettati llyee ahf·feht·tah·tee	cold cuts [charcuterie]
l'agliata lah·llyah·tah	garlic sauce
l'aglio lah·llyoh	garlic
l'agnello lah·nyehl·loh	lamb
gli agnolotti llyee ah·nyoh·loht·tee	meat-stuffed pasta
l'albicocca lahl·bee·kohk·kah	apricot

l'albume lahl·<u>boo</u>·meh	egg white
gli alcolici llyee ahl·<u>koh</u>·lee·chee	spirits
l'alloro lahl·<u>loh</u>·roh	bay leaf
l'amarena lah·mah·<u>reh</u>·nah	sour cherry
l'ananas <u>lah</u>·nah·nahs	pineapple
l'anatra <u>lah</u>·nah·trah	duck
l'aneto lah·<u>neh</u>·toh	dill
l'anguilla lahn·<u>gweel</u>·lah	eel
l'anguria lahn·<u>goo</u>·ryah	watermelon (northern Italy)
l'aperitivo lah·peh·ree·<u>tee</u>·voh	aperitif
l'arachide lah·<u>rah</u>·kee·deh	peanut
l'aragosta lah·rah·<u>goh</u>·stah	lobster
l'arancia lah·<u>rahn</u>·chyah	orange
l'aringa lah·<u>reen</u>·gah	herring
l'arrosto lahr·<u>roh</u>·stoh	roast
gli aromi llyee ah·<u>roh</u>·mee	herbs
l'asparago lah·<u>spah</u>·rah·goh	asparagus
l'avocado lah·voh·<u>kah</u>·doh	avocado
il baccalà eel bahk·kah·<u>lah</u>	salted, dried cod
la banana lah bah·<u>nah</u>·nah	banana
la barbabietola lah bahr·bah·<u>byeh</u>·toh·lah	beet
il basilico eel bah·<u>see</u>·lee·koh	basil
la bibita lah <u>bee</u>·bee·tah	soda
la bietola lah <u>byeh</u>·toh·lah	swiss chard
la birra lah <u>beer</u>·rah	beer
il biscotto eel bee·<u>skoht</u>·toh	cookie [biscuit]
la bistecca lah bee·<u>stehk</u>·kah	steak

la braciola lah brah·<u>chyoh</u>·lah	grilled pork chop
il brandy eel <u>brahn</u>·dee	brandy
il branzino eel brahn·<u>dzee</u>·noh	sea bass
i broccoli ee <u>brohk</u>·koh·lee	broccoli
il brodo eel <u>broh</u>·doh	broth
il budino eel boo·<u>dee</u>·noh	pudding
il bue eel <u>boo</u>·eh	ox
la burrida lah boo·<u>reed</u>·dah	fish stew (Genova)
il burro eel <u>boor</u>·roh	butter
il caffè eel kahf·<u>feh</u>	coffee
i calamari ee kah·lah·<u>mah</u>·ree	squid
la cannella lah kahn·<u>nehl</u>·lah	cinnamon
i cannelloni ee kahn·nehl·<u>loh</u>·nee	stuffed pasta tubes, topped with sauce and baked
i capelli d'angelo ee kah·<u>pehl</u>·lee dahn·<u>geh</u>·loh	angelhair pasta
i cappelletti ee kahp·pehl·<u>leht</u>·tee	small ravioli, filled with meat, ham, cheese and eggs
il cappero eel <u>kahp</u>·peh·roh	caper
la capra lah <u>kah</u>·prah	goat
il capretto eel kah·<u>preht</u>·toh	kid (baby goat)
le caramelle leh kah·rah·<u>mehl</u>·leh	candy [sweets]
il caramello eel kah·rah·<u>mehl</u>·loh	caramel
il carciofo eel kahr·<u>chyoh</u>·foh	artichoke
i cardi ee <u>kahr</u>·dee	cardoons (relative of the artichoke)
la carne lah <u>kahr</u>·neh	meat

la carne in scatola lah <u>kahr</u>·neh een <u>skah</u>·toh·lah — corned beef

la carne tritata lah <u>kahr</u>·neh tree·<u>tah</u>·tah — ground meat

la carota lah kah·<u>roh</u>·tah — carrot

la castagna lah kah·<u>stah</u>·nyah — chestnut

il cavolfiore eel kah·vohl·<u>fyoh</u>·reh — cauliflower

i cavoletti di Bruxelles ee kah·voh·<u>leht</u>·tee dee broo·<u>ksehl</u> — Brussels sprouts

il cavolo eel <u>kah</u>·voh·loh — cabbage

il cavolo rosso eel <u>kah</u>·voh·loh <u>rohs</u>·soh — red cabbage

i ceci ee <u>cheh</u>·chee — chickpeas

il cedro eel <u>cheh</u>·droh — lime

i cereali ee cheh·reh·<u>ah</u>·lee — cereal

il cervo eel <u>chehr</u>·voh — venison

il cetriolino eel cheh·tryoh·<u>lee</u>·noh — gherkin

il cetriolo eel cheh·<u>tryoh</u>·loh — cucumber

la ciambella fritta lah chahm·<u>behl</u>·lah <u>freet</u>·tah — doughnut

il chiodo di garofano eel <u>kyoh</u>·doh dee gah·<u>roh</u>·fah·noh — clove

la cicoria lah chee·<u>koh</u>·ryah — chicory

la ciliegia lah chee·<u>lyeh</u>·jyah — cherry

il cinghiale eel cheen·<u>ghyah</u>·leh — wild boar

il cioccolato eel chyohk·koh·<u>lah</u>·toh — chocolate

la cipolla lah chee·<u>pohl</u>·lah — onion

la cipollina verde lah chee·pohl·<u>lee</u>·nah <u>vehr</u>·deh — scallion [spring onion]

il cocco eel <u>kohk</u>·koh — coconut

il cocomero eel koh·<u>koh</u>·meh·roh — watermelon (Rome and southern Italy)

la coda di bue lah koh·dah dee boo·eh	oxtail
la confettura lah kohn·feht·too·rah	jam
il coniglio eel koh·nee·llyoh	rabbit
la conserva lah kohn·sehr·vah	tomato paste
il consommé eel kohn·sohm·meh	consommé
la coppa lah kohp·pah	cured pork shoulder
il cornetto eel kohr·neht·toh	croissant
la coscia lah koh·shah	leg
le cozze leh koh·tseh	mussel
il cracker eel krah·kehr	cracker
i crauti ee krawoo·tee	sauerkraut
la crema lah kreh·mah	custard
il crescione eel kreh·shyoh·neh	watercress
le crespelle leh kreh·spehl·leh	crepes
la crostata lah kroh·stah·tah	pie
il cumino eel koo·mee·noh	caraway/cumin
i datteri ee daht·teh·ree	dates
il digestivo eel dee·jeh·stee·voh	after-dinner drink
il dolcificante eel dohl·chee·fee·kahn·teh	sweetener
il dragoncello eel drah·gohn·chehl·loh	tarragon
l'erba cipollina lehr·bah chee·pohl·lee·nah	chives
l'erbetta lehr·beht·teh	herb
l'espresso leh·sprehs·soh	coffee
il fagiano eel fah·jyah·noh	pheasant
il fagiolino eel fah·jyoh·lee·noh	green bean
i fagioli di soya ee fah·jyoh·dee soh·yah	soybean [soya bean]
il fagiolo eel fah·jyoh·loh	bean
la faraona lah fah·rah·oh·nah	guinea fowl
la farina lah fah·ree·nah	flour

la farina d'avena lah fah·<u>ree</u>·nah dah·<u>veh</u>·nah	oatmeal
la farina di mais lah fah·<u>ree</u>·nah dee <u>mah</u>·ees	cornmeal
il fegato eel <u>feh</u>·gah·toh	liver
le fettuccine leh feht·too·<u>chee</u>·neh	egg noodles
il filetto eel fee·<u>leht</u>·toh	filet
il fico eel <u>fee</u>·koh	fig
il finocchio eel fee·<u>nohk</u>·kyoh	fennel
il formaggio eel fohr·<u>mah</u>·djoh	cheese
il formaggio caprino eel fohr·<u>mah</u>·djoh kah·<u>pree</u>·noh	goat cheese
il formaggio cremoso eel fohr·<u>mah</u>·djoh kreh·<u>moh</u>·zoh	cream cheese
i fiocchi di latte ee <u>fyohk</u>·kee dee <u>laht</u>·teh	cottage cheese
la fragola lah <u>frah</u>·goh·lah	strawberry
la frittata lah freet·<u>tah</u>·tah	omelet
la frittella lah freet·<u>tehl</u>·lah	fritter/pancake
il frullatto eel frool·<u>lah</u>·toh	milkshake
la frutta lah <u>froot</u>·tah	fruit
la frutta cotta lah <u>froot</u>·tah <u>koht</u>·tah	stewed fruit
i frutti di bosco ee <u>froot</u>·tee dee <u>boh</u>·skoh	mixed berries
i frutti di mare ee <u>froot</u>·tee dee <u>mah</u>·reh	seafood/shellfish
il fungo eel <u>foon</u>·goh	mushroom
i fusilli ee foo·<u>seel</u>·lee	spiral-shaped pasta
la gallina lah gahl·<u>lee</u>·nah	hen
il gambero eel <u>gahm</u>·beh·roh	shrimp
la gelatina lah jeh·lah·<u>tee</u>·nah	jelly
il gelato eel jeh·<u>lah</u>·toh	ice cream

il germoglio di soia eel jehr·<u>moh</u>·llyoh dee <u>soh</u>·yah		bean sprouts
il ghiaccio eel <u>ghyah</u>·chyoh		ice (cube)
il gin eel geen		gin
gli gnocchi llyee <u>nyohk</u>·kee		potato dumplings
il gorgonzola eel gohr·gohn·<u>dzoh</u>·lah		blue cheese
il granchio eel <u>grahn</u>·kyoh		crab
il grano eel <u>grah</u>·noh		wheat
la guava lah <u>gwah</u>·vah		guava
l'hamburger lahm·<u>boor</u>·gehr		hamburger
l'indivia leen·<u>dee</u>·vyah		endive
l'insalata leen·sah·<u>lah</u>·tah		salad
il ketchup eel <u>keht</u>·choop		ketchup
il kiwi eel <u>kee</u>·wee		kiwi
il lampone eel lahm·<u>poh</u>·neh		raspberry
le lasagne leh lah·<u>sah</u>·nyeh		lasagna
il latte eel <u>laht</u>·teh		milk
il latte di soia eel <u>laht</u>·teh dee <u>soh</u>·yah		soymilk [soya milk]
la lattuga lah laht·<u>too</u>·gah		lettuce
la lenticchia lah lehn·<u>teek</u>·kyah		lentil
la limonata lah lee·moh·<u>nah</u>·tah		lemon soda
il limone eel lee·<u>moh</u>·neh		lemon
le linguine leh leen·<u>gwee</u>·neh		flat noodles
la lingua lah <u>leen</u>·gwah		tongue
il liquore eel lee·<u>kwoh</u>·reh		liqueur
il liquore all'arancia eel lee·<u>kwoh</u>·reh <u>ahl</u>·lah·<u>rahn</u>·chyah		orange liqueur
il lombo eel <u>lohm</u>·boh		loin/sirloin
la lumaca lah loo·<u>mah</u>·kah		snail
i maccheroni ee mahk·keh·<u>roh</u>·nee		macaroni

il maiale eel mah·yah·leh — pork

il maialino da latte eel mah·yah·lee·noh dah laht·teh — suckling pig

la maionese lah mah·yoh·neh·zeh — mayonnaise

il mais dolce eel mah·ees dohl·cheh — sweet corn

il mandarino eel mahn·dah·ree·noh — tangerine

la mandorla lah mahn·dohr·lah — almond

il mango eel mahn·goh — mango

il manzo eel mahn·dzoh — beef

la margarina lah mahr·gah·ree·nah — margarine

la marmellata lah mahr·mehl·lah·tah — marmalade/jam

il marzapane eel mahr·dzah·pah·neh — marzipan

la mela lah meh·lah — apple

la melanzana lah meh·lahn·tsah·nah — eggplant [aubergine]

il melograno eel meh·loh·grah·noh — pomegranate

il melone eel meh·loh·neh — melon

la menta lah mehn·tah — mint

la merenda lah meh·rehn·dah — snack

la meringa lah meh·reen·gah — meringue

il merluzzo eel mehr·loo·tsoh — cod

il miele eel myeh·leh — honey

il minestrone eel mee·neh·stroh·neh — vegetable and bean soup

il mirtillo eel meer·teel·loh — blueberry

il montone eel mohn·toh·neh — mutton

la mora lah moh·rah — blackberry

la mortadella lah mohr·tah·dehl·lah — Bologna sausage

il muesli eel mweh·slee — granola [muesli]

il muffin eel mahf·feen — muffin

il nasello eel nah-<u>zehl</u>-loh	hake
la nocciola lah noh-<u>chyoh</u>-lah	hazelnut
la noce lah <u>noh</u>-cheh	walnut
la noce moscata lah <u>noh</u>-cheh moh-<u>skah</u>-tah	nutmeg
la nutella lah noo-<u>tehl</u>-lah	hazelnut-flavored chocolate spread
l'oca <u>loh</u>-kah	goose
l'olio d'oliva <u>loh</u>-lyoh doh-<u>lee</u>-vah	olive oil
l'oliva loh-<u>lee</u>-vah	olive
l'orata loh-<u>rah</u>-tah	sea bream
le orecchiette leh oh-rehk-<u>kyeht</u>-teh	small, shell-shaped pasta
l'origano loh-<u>ree</u>-gah-noh	oregano
l'ortaggio lohr-<u>tah</u>-djoh	vegetable
l'orzo <u>lohr</u>-tsoh	barley
l'ostrica <u>loh</u>-stree-kah	oyster
il palombo eel pah-<u>lohm</u>-boh	dogfish
la pancetta lah pahn-<u>cheht</u>-tah	bacon
il pane eel <u>pah</u>-neh	brcad
il pane tostato eel <u>pah</u>-neh toh-<u>stah</u>-toh	toast
il panino eel pah-<u>nee</u>-noh	roll/sandwich
la panna acida lah <u>pahn</u>-nah <u>ah</u>-chee-dah	sour cream
la panna montata lah <u>pahn</u>-nah mohn-<u>tah</u>-tah	whipped cream
la papaya lah pah-<u>pah</u>-yah	papaya
la pasta lah <u>pah</u>-stah	pastry
il pasticcio pah-<u>stee</u>-chyoh	pie
la pastina lah pah-<u>stee</u>-nah	tiny dried pasta used in soups

la patata lah pah·<u>tah</u>·tah	potato
la patata americana lah pah·<u>tah</u>·tah ah·meh·ree·<u>kah</u>·nah	sweet potato
le patatine leh pah·tah·<u>tee</u>·neh	potato chips [crisps]
le patatine fritte leh pah·tah·<u>tee</u>·neh <u>freet</u>·teh	French fries
il paté eel pah·<u>teh</u>	pâté
le penne leh <u>pehn</u>·neh	tubular pasta with angled ends
il pepe eel <u>peh</u>·peh	pepper (seasoning)
il pepe bianco eel <u>peh</u>·peh <u>byahn</u>·koh	white pepper (seasoning)
il pepe nero eel <u>peh</u>·peh <u>neh</u>·roh	black pepper (seasoning)
il pepe rosso eel <u>peh</u>·peh <u>rohs</u>·soh	paprika
il peperoncino eel peh·peh·rohn·<u>chee</u>·noh	chili pepper
il peperone eel peh·peh·<u>roh</u>·neh	pepper (vegetable)
la pera lah <u>peh</u>·rah	pear
il persico eel pehr·<u>see</u>·koh	fresh water perch
la pesca lah <u>peh</u>·skah	peach
il pesce eel <u>peh</u>·sheh	fish
il pesce spada eel <u>peh</u>·sheh <u>spah</u>·dah	swordfish
il pettine di mare eel peht·<u>tee</u>·neh dee <u>mah</u>·reh	scallop
il petto (di pollo) eel <u>peht</u>·toh (dee <u>pohl</u>·loh)	breast (of chicken)
i pinoli ee pee·<u>noh</u>·lee	pine nuts
il piselli eel pee·<u>zehl</u>·lee	peas
il pesto eel <u>peh</u>·stoh	sauce made with basil, garlic, parmesan and pine nuts
la pizza lah <u>pee</u>·tsah	pizza

il pollame eel pohl·<u>lah</u>·meh	poultry
il pollo eel <u>pohl</u>·loh	chicken
la polenta lah poh·<u>lehn</u>·tah	cornmeal
la polpa di granchio lah <u>pohl</u>·pah dee <u>grahn</u>·kyoh	crabmeat
la polpetta lah pohl·<u>peht</u>·tah	meatball
il polpo eel <u>pohl</u>·poh	octopus
il pomodoro eel poh·moh·<u>doh</u>·roh	tomato
il pompelmo eel pohm·<u>pehl</u>·moh	grapefruit
i porcini ee pohr·<u>chee</u>·nee	porcini mushrooms
la porchetta lah pohr·<u>keht</u>·tah	suckling pig
il porro eel <u>pohr</u>·roh	leek
il porto eel <u>pohr</u>·toh	port
il prezzemolo eel preh·<u>tseh</u>·moh·loh	parsley
il prosciutto eel proh·<u>shyoot</u>·toh	ham
la prugna lah <u>proo</u>·nyah	plum
la prugna secca lah <u>proo</u>·nyah <u>sehk</u>·kah	prune
le puntarelle leh poon·tah·<u>rehl</u>·leh	wild chicory
i quadrucci ee kwah·<u>droo</u>·chee	stuffed pasta squares added to soup
la quaglia lah <u>kwah</u>·llyah	quail
il rabarbaro eel rah·<u>bahr</u>·bah·roh	rhubarb
il radicchio eel rah·<u>deek</u>·kyoh	red chicory
il ravanello eel rah·vah·<u>nehl</u>·loh	radish
la rana lah <u>rah</u>·nah	frog
la rana pescatrice lah <u>rah</u>·nah peh·skah·<u>tree</u>·cheh	monkfish
la rapa lah <u>rah</u>·pah	turnip
il ribes nero eel <u>ree</u>·behs <u>neh</u>·roh	black currant
il ribes rosso eel <u>ree</u>·behs <u>rohs</u>·soh	red currant

il riccio di mare eel <u>ree</u>·chyoh dee <u>mah</u>·reh — sea urchin

le rigaglie leh ree·<u>gah</u>·llyeh — giblet

i rigatoni ee ree·gah·<u>toh</u>·nee — fat, ridged tubes of dried pasta with ridges

il riso eel <u>ree</u>·zoh — rice

il risotto eel ree·<u>zoht</u>·toh — rice cooked in broth

il rosbif eel <u>rohz</u>·beef — roast beef

il rosmarino eel rohz·mah·<u>ree</u>·noh — rosemary

il rum eel room — rum

il salame eel sah·<u>lah</u>·meh — salami

il sale eel <u>sah</u>·leh — salt

il salmone eel sahl·<u>moh</u>·neh — salmon

la salsa lah <u>sahl</u>·sah — sauce

la salsa agrodolce lah <u>sahl</u>·sah ah·groh·<u>dohl</u>·cheh — sweet and sour sauce

la salsa piccante lah <u>sahl</u>·sah peek·<u>kahn</u>·teh — hot pepper sauce

la salsa di soia lah <u>sahl</u>·sah dee <u>soh</u>·yah — soy sauce

la salsiccia lah sahl·<u>see</u>·chyah — sausage

la salvia lah <u>sahl</u>·vyah — sage

il sanguinaccio eel sahn·gwee·<u>nah</u>·chyoh — blood sausage

le sardine leh sahr·<u>dee</u>·neh — sardine

i savoiardi ee sah·voh·<u>yahr</u>·dee — "ladyfingers", small sponge cakes used to make tiramisu

lo scalogno loh skah·<u>loh</u>·nyoh — shallot

la scarola lah skah·<u>roh</u>·lah — escarole

lo sciroppo loh shee·<u>rohp</u>·poh — syrup

lo scotch loh skohtch — scotch

il sedano eel <u>seh</u>·dah·noh — celery

la segale lah seh·<u>gah</u>·leh — rye

la selvaggina lah sehl·vah·djee·nah	game
i semi di finocchio ee seh·mee dee fee·nohk·kyoh	fennel seeds
la senape lah seh·nah·peh	mustard
lo scombro loh skohm·broh	mackerel
lo sherry loh shehr·ree	sherry
la sogliola lah soh·llyoh·lah	sole
la soia lah soh·yah	soy [soya]
il sottaceto eel soht·tah·cheh·toh	pickle
gli spaghetti llyee spah·gheht·tee	spaghetti
la spalla lah spahl·lah	shoulder
le spezie leh speh·tsyeh	spices
lo spezzatino loh speh·tsah·tee·noh	meat stew
gli spinaci llyee spee·nah·chee	spinach
la spremuta lah spreh·muh·tah	fresh-squeezed juice
lo stinco loh stccn·koh	shank
lo strutto loh stroot·toh	lard
il succo eel sook·koh	juice
il tacchino eel tahk·kee·noh	turkey
la tagliatella lah tah·llyah·tehl·lah	noodle
il tartufo eel tahr·too·foh	truffles
il tè eel teh	tea
il timo eel tee·moh	thyme
il tofu eel toh·foo	tofu
il tonno eel tohn·noh	tuna
il torrone eel tohr·roh·neh	nougat
la torta lah tohr·tah	cake
i tortelli ee tohr·tehl·lee	fat, elongated, stuffed ravioli

i tortellini ee tohr·tehl·<u>lee</u>·nee	small stuffed pasta nuggets
la triglia lah <u>tree</u>·llyah	red mullet
la trippa lah <u>treep</u>·pah	tripe
la trota lah <u>troh</u>·tah	trout
il tuorlo eel <u>twohr</u>·loh	egg yolk
l'uovo <u>lwoh</u>·voh	egg
l'uva <u>loo</u>·vah	grape
l'uva spina <u>loo</u>·vah <u>spee</u>·nah	gooseberry
l'uvetta loo·<u>veht</u>·tah	raisin
la vaniglia lah vah·<u>nee</u>·llyah	vanilla
il vermouth eel <u>vehr</u>·mooth	vermouth
la verdura lah vehr·<u>doo</u>·rah	vegetable
il vino eel <u>vee</u>·noh	wine
il vino da dessert eel <u>vee</u>·noh dah dehs·<u>sehrt</u>	dessert wine
il vitello eel vee·<u>tehl</u>·loh	veal
la vodka lah <u>vohd</u>·kah	vodka
la vongola lah <u>vohn</u>·goh·lah	clam
il wafer eel <u>vah</u>·fehr	waffle
il whisky eel <u>whee</u>·skee	whisky
il wurstel eel <u>voor</u>·stehl	hot dog
lo yogurt loh <u>yoh</u>·goort	yogurt
lo zafferano loh dzahf·feh·<u>rah</u>·noh	saffron
lo zenzero loh <u>dzehn</u>·dzeh·roh	ginger
gli ziti llyee <u>tsee</u>·tee	tubular pasta
la zucca lah <u>dzook</u>·kah	squash
lo zucchero loh <u>dzook</u>·keh·roh	sugar
la zucchina lah <u>dzook</u>·kee·nah	zucchini [courgette]
la zuppa lah <u>dzoop</u>·pah	soup

▼ *People*

Essential

Hello!	**Salve!** <u>sahl</u>·veh
Hi!	**Ciao!** <u>chah</u>·oh
How are you?	**Come sta?** <u>koh</u>·meh stah
Fine, thanks.	**Bene, grazie.** <u>beh</u>·neh <u>grah</u>·tsyeh
Excuse me!	**Scusi!** <u>skoo</u>·zee
Do you speak English?	**Parla inglese?** <u>pahr</u>·lah een·<u>gleh</u>·zeh
What's your name?	**Come si chiama?** <u>koh</u>·meh see <u>kyah</u>·mah
My name is…	**Mi chiamo…** mee <u>kyah</u>·moh…
Nice to meet you.	**Piacere.** pyah·<u>cheh</u>·reh
Where are you from?	**Di dov'è?** dee doh·<u>veh</u>
I'm American.	**Sono americano♂/americana♀.** <u>soh</u>·noh ah·meh·ree·<u>kah</u>·noh♂/ah·meh·ree·<u>kah</u>·nah♀
I'm British.	**Sono inglese.** <u>soh</u>·noh een·<u>gleh</u>·zeh
What do you do?	**Cosa fa?** <u>koh</u>·zah fah
I work for…	**Lavoro per…** lah·<u>voh</u>·roh pehr…
I'm a student.	**Studio.** <u>stoo</u>·dyoh
I'm retired.	**Sono in pensione.** <u>soh</u>·noh een pehn·<u>syoh</u>·neh
Do you like…?	**Le piace…?** leh <u>pyah</u>·cheh…
Goodbye.	**Arrivederla.** ahr·ree·veh·<u>dehr</u>·lah
See you later.	**A dopo.** ah <u>doh</u>·poh

Italians have many greetings. The following are the most commonly used forms and when to use them.

buongiorno: literally, good day; this greeting is used from morning to mid-afternoon
salve: a formal hello
ciao: an informal hi or bye
buon pomeriggio: good afternoon
buonasera: good evening; used from late afternoon until late in the evening
buonanotte: good night; used late in the evening or at bedtime
arrivederla: formal goodbye
arrivederci: informal goodbye

Signore (Mr.), **Signora** (Mrs.), **Signorina** (Miss) and professional titles—**Dottore** (Dr.), **Professore** (Professor)—are frequently used, even when you don't know the person's last name. When trying to get someone's attention, you don't have to include his or her title; a simple **Scusi!** (formal) or **Scusa!** (informal) is sufficient.

Communication Difficulties

Do you speak English?	**Parla inglese?** pahr·lah een·gleh·zeh
Does anyone here speak English?	**Qualcuno parla inglese?** kwahl·koo·noh pahr·lah een·gleh·zeh
I don't speak (much) Italian.	**Non parlo (molto bene l') italiano.** nohn pahr·loh (mohl·toh beh·neh l) ee·tah·lyah·noh
Can you speak more slowly?	**Può parlare più lentamente?** pwoh pahr·lah·reh pyoo lehn·tah·mehn·teh
Can you repeat that?	**Può ripetere?** pwoh ree·peh·teh·reh
Excuse me?	**Come?** koh·meh

What was that?	**Cosa ha detto?** <u>koh</u>·zah ah <u>deht</u>·toh
Can you spell it?	**Come si scrive?** <u>koh</u>·meh see <u>skree</u>·veh
Can you write it down?	**Me lo può scrivere?** meh loh pwo <u>skree</u>·veh·reh
Can you translate this into English for me?	**Può tradurlo in inglese?** pwoh trah·<u>door</u>·loh een een·<u>gleh</u>·zeh
What does… mean?	**Che significa…?** keh see·<u>nyee</u>·fee·kah…
I understand.	**Capisco.** kah·<u>pee</u>·skoh
I don't understand.	**Non capisco.** nohn kah·<u>pee</u>·skoh
Do you understand?	**Capisce?** kah·<u>pee</u>·sheh

You May Hear…

Parlo poco inglese. <u>pahr</u>·loh <u>poh</u>·koh een·<u>gleh</u>·zeh	I only speak a little English.
Non parlo inglese. nohn <u>pahr</u>·loh een·<u>gleh</u>·zeh	I don't speak English.

Making Friends

Hello!	**Salve!** <u>sahl</u>·veh
Good morning.	**Buongiorno.** bwohn·<u>jyohr</u>·noh
Good afternoon.	**Buon pomeriggio.** bwohn poh·meh·<u>ree</u>·djoh
Good evening.	**Buonasera.** bwoh·nah·<u>seh</u>·rah
My name is…	**Mi chiamo…** mee <u>kyah</u>·moh…
What's your name?	**Come si chiama?** <u>koh</u>·meh see <u>kyah</u>·mah
I'd like to introduce you to…	**Le presento…** leh preh·<u>zehn</u>·toh…
Pleased to meet you.	**Piacere.** pyah·<u>cheh</u>·reh
How are you?	**Come sta?** <u>koh</u>·meh stah
Fine, thanks. And you?	**Bene, grazie. E Lei?** <u>beh</u>·neh <u>grah</u>·tsyeh eh lay

A handshake is a common gesture among strangers or in
formal settings. Traditionally, it is expected that a woman
be the first to offer her hand. A kiss on both cheeks is used
among friends and relatives. A nod and a smile suffice when
greeting members of a group of people.

Travel Talk

I'm here…	**Sono qui…** <u>soh</u>·noh kwee…
– on business	**– per lavoro** pehr lah·<u>voh</u>·roh
– on vacation [holiday]	**– in vacanza** een vah·<u>kahn</u>·tsah
– studying	**– per studio** pehr <u>stoo</u>·dyoh

I'm staying for…	**Rimango…** ree·<u>mahn</u>·goh…
I've been here…	**Sono qui da…** soh·noh kwee dah…
– a day	**– un giorno** oon <u>jyohr</u>·noh
– a week	**– una settimana** <u>oo</u>·nah seht·tee·<u>mah</u>·nah
– a month	**– un mese** oon <u>meh</u>·zeh

▶ For numbers, see page 177.

| Where are you from? | **Di dov'è?** dee doh·<u>veh</u> |

Relationships

Who are you with?	**Con chi è?** kohn kee ee
I'm here alone.	**Sono da solo** ♂ **/sola** ♀. <u>soh</u>·noh dah <u>soh</u>·loh ♂ /<u>soh</u>·lah ♀
I'm with my…	**Sono con…** <u>soh</u>·noh kohn…
– husband/wife	**– mio marito** ♂ **/mia moglie** ♀ <u>mee</u>·oh mah·<u>ree</u>·toh ♂ /<u>mee</u>·ah <u>moh</u>·llyeh ♀
– boyfriend/ girlfriend	**– il mio ragazzo** ♂ **/la mia ragazza** ♀ eel <u>mee</u>·oh rah·<u>gah</u>·tsoh ♂ /lah <u>mee</u>·ah rah·<u>gah</u>·tsah ♀
– friend	**– un amico** ♂ **/ un'amica** ♀ oon ah·<u>mee</u>·koh ♂ /oo·nah·<u>mee</u>·kah ♀
– friends	**– degli amici** ♂ **/delle amiche** ♀ <u>deh</u>·llyee ah·<u>mee</u>·chee ♂ /<u>dehl</u>·leh ah·<u>mee</u>·keh ♀
– colleague	**– un** ♂ **/una** ♀ **collega** oon ♂ /<u>oo</u>·nah ♀ kohl·<u>leh</u>·gah
– colleagues	**– dei colleghi** ♂ **/delle colleghe** ♀ day kohl·<u>leh</u>·ghee ♂ /<u>deh</u>·leh kohl·<u>leh</u>·gheh ♀

When's your birthday?	**Quando è il suo compleanno?** kwahn-doh eh eel soo-oh kohm-pleh-ahn-noh
How old are you?	**Quanti anni ha?** kwahn-tee ahn-nee ah
I'm…years old.	**Ho…anni.** oh…ahn-nee

▶For numbers, see page 177.

Are you married?	**È sposato♂/sposata♀?** eh spoh-zah-toh♂/ spoh-zah-tah♀
I'm…	**Sono…** soh-noh…
– single	– **single** seen-guhl
– widowed	– **vedovo♂/vedova♀** veh-doh-voh♂/ veh-doh-vah♀
– married	– **sposato♂/sposata♀** spoh-zah-toh♂/ spoh-zah-tah♀
– divorced	– **divorziato♂/ divorziata♀** dee-vohr-tsyah-toh♂/dee-vohr-tsyah-tah♀
– separated	– **separato♂/separata♀** seh-pah-rah-toh♂/ seh-pah-rah-tah♀
I have a boyfriend/girlfriend.	**Ho *un ragazzo/una ragazza.*** oh oon rah-gah-tsoh/oo-nah rah-gah-tsah
Do you have children/ grandchildren?	**Ha *figli/nipoti*?** ah fee-llyee/nee-poh-tee

Work and School ─────────────

What do you do?	**Cosa fa?** koh-zah fah
What are you studying?	**Cosa studia?** koh-zah stoo-dyah
I'm studying Italian.	**Studio italiano.** stoo-dyoh ee-tah-lyah-noh

I...	Io... ee·oh...
– work *full-time/* *part-time*	– **lavoro *full-time/part-time*** lah·voh·roh *fool·tym/pahrt·tym*
– am unemployed	– **sono disoccupato**♂**/disoccupata**♀ soh·noh dee·zohk·koo·pah·toh ♂/dee·zohk·koo·pah·tah ♀
– work at home	– **lavoro a casa** lah·voh·roh ah kah·zah
Who do you work for?	**Per chi lavora?** pehr kee lah·voh·rah
I work for...	**Lavoro per...** lah·voh·roh pehr...
Here's my business card.	**Ecco il mio biglietto da visita.** ehk·koh eel mee·oh bee·llyeht·toh dah vee·zee·tah

▶ For business travel, see page 149.

Weather

What's the forecast?	**Come sono le previsioni?** koh·meh soh·noh leh preh·vee·zyoh·nee
What *beautiful/* *terrible* weather!	**Che *bel/brutto* tempo!** keh *behl/broot·toh* tehm·poh
It's *cool/warm*.	**Fa *fresco/caldo*.** fah *freh·skoh/kahl·doh*
It's *cold/hot*.	**Fa *freddo/caldo*.** fah *frehd·doh/kahl·doh*
It's rainy.	**Piove.** pyoh·veh
It's sunny.	**C'è il sole.** cheh eel soh·leh
It's snowy.	**Nevica.** neh·vee·kah
It's icy.	**Gela.** jeh·lah
Do I need *a jacket/an umbrella*?	**Devo prendere *una giacca/un ombrello*?** deh·voh prehn·deh·reh *oo·nah jyahk·kah/oon ohm·brehl·loh*

▶ For temperature, see page 183.

Romance

Essential

Would you like to go out for *a drink/dinner*?	**Le va di andare a *bere qualcosa/cena*?** leh vah dee ahn·<u>dah</u>·reh ah *beh·reh kwahl·<u>koh</u>·zah/<u>cheh</u>·nah*
What are your plans for *tonight/tomorrow*?	**Che programmi ha per *stasera/domani*?** keh proh·<u>grahm</u>·mee <u>ah</u> pehr *stah·<u>seh</u>·rah/doh·<u>mah</u>·nee*
Can I have your number?	**Mi dà il suo numero?** mee dah eel <u>soo</u>·oh <u>noo</u>·meh·roh
Can I get you a drink?	**Posso offrirle qualcosa?** <u>pohs</u>·soh ohf·<u>freer</u>·leh kwahl·<u>koh</u>·zah
I like you.	**Mi piaci.** mee <u>pyah</u>·chee
I love you.	**Ti amo.** tee <u>ah</u>·moh

Making Plans

Would you like to go out for *a coffee/drink*?	**Le va di andare a prendere un *caffè/bicchierino*?** leh vah dee ahn·<u>dah</u>·reh ah <u>prehn</u>·deh·reh oon *kahf·<u>feh</u>/bee·kyeh·<u>ree</u>·noh*
Would you like to go to dinner?	**Le va di andare a cena?** leh vah dee ahn·<u>dah</u>·reh ah <u>cheh</u>·nah
What are your plans for…?	**Che programmi ha per…?** keh proh·<u>grahm</u>·mee ah pehr…
– tonight	**– stasera** stah·<u>seh</u>·rah
– tomorrow	**– domani** doh·<u>mah</u>·nee
– this weekend	**– questo weekend** <u>kweh</u>·stoh week·<u>ehnd</u>
Where would you like to go?	**Dove le va di andare?** <u>doh</u>·veh leh vah dee ahn·<u>dah</u>·reh
I'd like to go to…	**Vorrei andare a…** vohr·<u>ray</u> ahn·<u>dah</u>·reh ah…

Do you like…?   **Le piace…?** leh <u>pyah</u>·cheh…

Can I have your   **Mi dà *il suo numero/la sua e-mail*?** mee
number/e-mail?   dah eel <u>soo</u>·oh <u>noo</u>·meh·roh/lah <u>soo</u>·ah <u>ee</u>-mayl

▶ For e-mail and phone, see page 47.

Pick-up [Chat-up] Lines

Can I sit here?	**Mi posso sedere?** mee pohs·soh seh·<u>deh</u>·reh
You're very attractive.	**È molto attraente.** eh <u>mohl</u>·toh aht·trah·<u>ehn</u>·teh
Let's go somewhere quieter.	**Andiamo in un posto più tranquillo.** ahn·<u>dyah</u>·moh een oon <u>poh</u>·stoh pyoo trahn·<u>kweel</u>·loh

Accepting and Rejecting

I'd love to.	**Mi piacerebbe moltissimo.** mee pyah·cheh·<u>rehb</u>·beh mohl·<u>tees</u>·see·moh
Where should we meet?	**Dove ci vediamo?** <u>doh</u>·veh chee veh·<u>dyah</u>·moh
I'll meet you at *the bar/your hotel*.	**Vediamoci *al bar/nel suo hotel*.** veh·<u>dyah</u>·moh·chee ahl bahr/nehl <u>soo</u>·oh oh·<u>tehl</u>
I'll come by at...	**Passo alle...** <u>pahs</u>·soh <u>ahl</u>·leh...

▶For time, see page 179.

What is your address?	**Mi dà il suo indirizzo?** mee dah eel <u>soo</u>·oh een·dee·<u>ree</u>·tsoh
I'm busy.	**Ho da fare.** oh dah <u>fah</u>·reh
I'm not interested.	**Non m'interessa.** nohn meen·teh·<u>rehs</u>·sah
Leave me alone.	**Mi lasci in pace.** mee <u>lah</u>·shee een <u>pah</u>·cheh
Stop bothering me!	**Smetta d'infastidirmi!** <u>smeht</u>·tah deen·<u>fah</u>·stee·<u>deer</u>·mee

Getting Physical

Can I *hug you/kiss you*?	**Posso *abbracciarti/baciarti*?** pohs-soh ahb-brah-*chyahr*-tee/bah-*chyahr*-tee
Yes.	**Sì.** see
No.	**No.** noh
Stop!	**Basta!** bah-stah
I like you.	**Mi piaci.** mee pyah-chee
I love you.	**Ti amo.** tee ah-moh

Sexual Preferences

Are you gay?	**Sei gay?** say gay
I'm...	**Sono...** soh-noh...
– heterosexual	**– eterosessuale** eh-teh-roh-sehs-swah-leh
– homosexual	**– omosessuale** oh-moh-sehs-swah-leh
– bisexual	**– bisex** bee-sehks
Do you like *men/women*?	**Ti piacciono *gli uomini/le donne*?** tee pyah-chyoh-noh *llyee woh-mee-nee/leh dohn-neh*

▼ *Fun*

Sightseeing

Essential

Where's the tourist information office?	**Dov'è l'ufficio informazioni turistiche?** doh·<u>veh</u> loof·<u>fee</u>·chyoh een·fohr·mah·<u>tsyoh</u>·nee too·<u>ree</u>·stee·keh
What are the main attractions?	**Cosa c'è da vedere?** <u>koh</u>·zah ceh dah veh·<u>deh</u>·reh
Do you have tours in English?	**Ci sono visite guidate in inglese?** chee <u>soh</u>·noh <u>vee</u>·zee·teh gwee·<u>dah</u>·teh een een·<u>gleh</u>·zeh
Can I have a *map/guide*?	**Mi può dare una *cartina/guida*?** mee pwoh <u>dah</u>·reh <u>oo</u>·nah *kahr·<u>tee</u>·nah/<u>gwee</u>·dah*

Tourist Information Office ────────────

Do you have information on...?	**Avete informazioni su...?** ah·<u>veh</u>·teh een·fohr·mah·<u>tsyoh</u>·nee soo...
Can you recommend...?	**Può consigliarmi...?** pwoh kohn·see·<u>llyahr</u>·mee...
– a bus tour	**– una gita in pullman** <u>oo</u>·nah <u>jee</u>·tah een <u>pool</u>·mahn
– an excursion to...	**– un'escursione a...** oo·neh·skoor·<u>syoh</u>·neh ah...
– a sightseeing tour	**– una gita turistica** <u>oo</u>·nah <u>jee</u>·tah too·<u>ree</u>·stee·kah

---

i **L'ufficio informazioni turistiche** (tourist information office) can be found in almost every town; some may be located at the airport or main train station. Get local events listings, maps, transportation schedules and more at any of these offices.

Tours

I'd like to go on the tour to…
Vorrei partecipare alla gita per… vohr·<u>ray</u> pahr·teh·chee·<u>pah</u>·reh ahl·lah <u>jee</u>·tah pehr…

When's the next tour?
Quando è la prossima gita? kwahn·doh eh lah <u>prohs</u>·see·mah <u>jee</u>·tah

Are there tours in English?
Ci sono visite guidate in inglese? chee <u>soh</u>·noh <u>vee</u>·zee·teh gwee·<u>dah</u>·teh een een·<u>gleh</u>·zeh

Is there an English *guide book/audio guide*?
C'è *una guida/un'audio guida* **in inglese?** cheh <u>oo</u>·nah <u>gwee</u>·dah/oo·<u>now</u>·dyoh <u>gwee</u>·dah een een·<u>gleh</u>·zeh

What time do we return?
A che ora si torna? ah keh <u>oh</u>·rah see <u>tohr</u>·nah

We'd like to see…
Vorremmo vedere… vohr·<u>rehm</u>·moh veh·<u>deh</u>·reh…

Can we stop here…?
Possiamo fermarci…? pohs·<u>syah</u>·moh fehr·<u>mahr</u>·chee…

– to take photos
– per fare qualche foto pehr <u>fah</u>·reh <u>kwahl</u>·keh <u>foh</u>·toh

– for souvenirs
– per comprare qualche souvenir pehr kohm·<u>prah</u>·reh <u>kwahl</u>·keh soo·veh·<u>neer</u>

– for the restrooms [toilets]
– per andare in bagno pehr ahn·<u>dah</u>·reh een <u>bah</u>·nyoh

Is it handicapped [disabled]-accessible?
È accessibile ai disabili? eh ah·chehs·<u>see</u>·bee·leh <u>ah</u>·ee dee·<u>zah</u>·bee·lee

▶For ticketing, see page 19.

118

Where is/Where are…?	**Dov'è/Dove sono…?** doh·<u>veh</u>/<u>doh</u>·veh <u>soh</u>·noh…
– the botanical garden	– **il giardino botanico** eel jyahr·<u>dee</u>·noh boh·<u>tah</u>·nee·koh
– the castle	– **il castello** eel kah·<u>stehl</u>·loh
– the downtown area	– **il centro** eel <u>chehn</u>·troh
– the fountain	– **la fontana** lah fohn·<u>tah</u>·nah
– the library	– **la biblioteca** lah bee·blyoh·<u>teh</u>·kah
– the market	– **il mercato** eel mehr·<u>kah</u>·toh
– the museum	– **il museo** eel moo·<u>zeh</u>·oh
– the old town	– **la città vecchia** lah cheet·<u>tah</u> <u>vehk</u>·kyah
– the opera house	– **il teatro dell'opera** eel teh·<u>ah</u>·troh deh·<u>loh</u>·peh·rah
– the palace	– **il palazzo** eel pah·<u>lah</u>·tsoh
– the park	– **il parco** eel <u>pahr</u>·koh
– the ruins	– **le rovine** leh roh·<u>vee</u>·neh
– the shopping area	– **i negozi** ee neh·<u>goh</u>·tzee
– the town hall	– **il comune** eel koh·<u>moo</u>·neh
– the town square	– **la piazza principale** lah <u>pyah</u>·tsah preen·chee·<u>pah</u>·leh
Can you show me on the map?	**Può indicarmelo sulla cartina?** pwoh een·dee·<u>kahr</u>·meh·loh <u>sool</u>·lah kahr·<u>tee</u>·nah

▶ For directions, see page 33.

Impressions

It's…   **È…** eh…

– amazing   – **meraviglioso** meh·rah·vee·<u>llyoh</u>·zoh

– beautiful   – **bellissimo** behl·<u>lees</u>·see·moh

– boring   – **noioso** noh·<u>yoh</u>·zoh

– interesting   – **interessante** een·teh·rehs·<u>sahn</u>·teh

– magnificent   – **magnifico** mah·<u>nyee</u>·fee·koh

– romantic   – **romantico** roh·<u>mahn</u>·tee·koh

– strange   – **strano** <u>strah</u>·noh

– stunning   – **fenomenale** feh·noh·meh·<u>nah</u>·leh

120

– terrible	**– terribile** tehr·<u>ree</u>·bee·leh
– ugly	**– brutto** <u>broot</u>·toh
I (don't) like it.	**(Non) Mi piace.** (nohn) mee <u>pyah</u>·cheh

Religion

Where's…?	**Dov'è…?** doh·<u>veh</u>…
– the cathedral	**– la cattedrale** lah kaht·teh·<u>drah</u>·leh
– the *Catholic/ Protestant* church	**– la chiesa *cattolica/protestante*** lah <u>kyeh</u>·zah *kaht·<u>toh</u>·lee·kah/proh·teh·<u>stahn</u>·teh*
– the mosque	**– la moschea** lah moh·<u>skeh</u>·ah
– the shrine	**– il santuario** eel sahn·<u>twah</u>·ryoh
– the synagogue	**– la sinagoga** lah see·nah·<u>goh</u>·gah
– the temple	**– il tempio** eel <u>tehm</u>·pyoh
What time is *the mass/service*?	**A che ora è *la messa/il servizio*?** ah keh <u>oh</u>·rah eh *lah <u>mehs</u>·sah/eel sehr·<u>vee</u>·tsyoh*

Shopping

Essential

Where's the *market/ mall [shopping centre]*?	**Dov'è il *mercato/centro commerciale*?** doh·<u>veh</u> eel *mehr·<u>kah</u>·toh/<u>chehn</u>·troh kohm·mehr·<u>chyah</u>·leh*
I'm just looking.	**Sto solo guardando.** stoh <u>soh</u>·loh gwahr·<u>dahn</u>·doh
Can you help me?	**Può aiutarmi?** pwoh ah·yoo·<u>tahr</u>·mee
I'm being helped.	**Mi stanno servendo.** mee <u>stahn</u>·noh sehr·<u>vehn</u>·doh
How much?	**Quant'è?** kwahn·<u>teh</u>

That one, please.	**Quello, per favore.** <u>kwehl</u>·loh pehr fah·<u>voh</u>·reh
That's all.	**Basta così.** <u>bah</u>·stah koh·<u>zee</u>
Where can I pay?	**Dove posso pagare?** <u>doh</u>·veh <u>pohs</u>·soh pah·<u>gah</u>·reh
I'll pay *in cash/by credit card.*	**Pago *in contanti/con carta di credito.*** <u>pah</u>·goh *een* kohn·<u>tahn</u>·tee/*kohn* <u>kahr</u>·tah *dee* <u>kreh</u>·dee·toh
A receipt, please.	**Una ricevuta, per favore.** <u>oo</u>·nah ree·cheh·<u>voo</u>·tah pehr fah·<u>voh</u>·reh

Stores

Where's…?	**Dov'è…?** doh·<u>veh</u>…
– the antiques store	**– un negozio di antiquariato** oon neh·<u>goh</u>·tsyoh dee ahn·tee·kwah·<u>ryah</u>·toh
– the bakery	**– una panetteria** oo·nah pah·neht·teh·<u>ree</u>·ah
– the bank	**– una banca** <u>oo</u>·nah <u>bahn</u>·kah
– the bookstore	**– una libreria** <u>oo</u>·nah lee·breh·<u>ree</u>·ah
– the camera store	**– un negozio di fotografia** oon neh·<u>goh</u>·tsyoh dee foh·toh·grah·<u>fee</u>·ah
– the clothing store	**– un negozio di abbigliamento** oon neh·<u>goh</u>·tsyoh dee ahb·bee·llyah·<u>mehn</u>·toh
– the delicatessen	**– un negozio di gastronomia** oon neh·<u>goh</u>·tsyoh dee gahs·troh·noh·<u>mee</u>·ah
– the department store	**– un grande magazzino** oon <u>grahn</u>·deh mah·gah·<u>dzee</u>·noh
– the gift shop	**– un negozio di oggettistica** oon neh·<u>goh</u>·tsyoh dee oh·djeht·<u>tee</u>·stee·kah
– the health food store	**– un'erboristeria** oo·nehr·boh·ree·steh·<u>ree</u>·ah

– the jeweler	– **una gioiellieria** <u>oo</u>·nah jyoh·yehl·lyeh·<u>ree</u>·ah
– the liquor store [off-licence]	– **un'enoteca** oo·neh·noh·<u>teh</u>·kah
– the market	– **un mercato** oon mehr·<u>kah</u>·toh
– the pastry shop	– **una pasticceria** <u>oo</u>·nah pah·stee·cheh·<u>ree</u>·ah
– the pharmacy [chemist]	– **una farmacia** <u>oo</u>·nah fahr·mah·<u>chee</u>·ah
– the produce [grocery] store	– **il fruttivendolo** eel froot·tee·vehn·<u>doh</u>·loh
– the shoe store	– **un negozio di calzature** oon neh·<u>goh</u>·tsyoh dee kahl·tsah·<u>too</u>·reh
– the shopping mall [shopping centre]	– **un centro commerciale** oon <u>chehn</u>·troh kohm·mehr·<u>chyah</u>·leh
– the souvenir store	– **un negozio di souvenir** oon neh·<u>goh</u>·tsyoh dee soo·veh·<u>neer</u>
– the supermarket	– **un supermercato** oon soo·pehr·mehr·<u>kah</u>·toh
– the tobacconist	– **un tabaccaio** oon tah·bahk·<u>kah</u>·yoh
– the toy store	– **un negozio di giocattoli** oon neh·<u>goh</u>·tsyoh dee jyoh·<u>kaht</u>·toh·lee

Services

Can you recommend...?	**Può consigliarmi...?** pwoh kohn·see·<u>llyahr</u>·mee...
– a barber	– **un barbiere** oon bahr·<u>byeh</u>·reh
– a dry cleaner	– **il lavasecco** eel lah·vah·<u>sehk</u>·koh
– a hairstylist	– **un parrucchiere** oon pahr·rook·<u>kyeh</u>·reh
– a laundromat [launderette]	– **una lavanderia a gettone** <u>oo</u>·nah lah·vahn·deh·<u>ree</u>·ah ah jeht·<u>toh</u>·neh
– a nail salon	– **un salone di bellezza** oon sah·<u>loh</u>·neh dee beh·<u>leh</u>·tsah
– a spa	– **una stazione termali** <u>oo</u>·nah stah·<u>tsyoh</u>·neh tehr·<u>mah</u>·lee
– a travel agency	– **un'agenzia di viaggi** oo·nah·jehn·<u>tsee</u>·ah dee <u>vyah</u>·djee
Can you...this?	**Mi può...questo♂/questa♀?** mee pwoh...<u>kweh</u>·stoh♂/<u>kweh</u>·stah♀
– alter	– **cambiare** kahm·<u>byah</u>·reh
– clean	– **pulire** poo·<u>lee</u>·reh
– fix [mend]	– **riparare** ree·pah·<u>rah</u>·reh
– press	– **stirare** stee·<u>rah</u>·reh
When will it be ready?	**Per quando è pronto♂/pronta♀?** pehr <u>kwahn</u>·doh eh <u>prohn</u>·toh♂/<u>prohn</u>·tah♀

Spa

I'd like...	**Vorrei fare...** vohr·<u>ray</u> <u>fah</u>·reh...
– a bikini wax	– **la ceretta all'inguine** lah cheh·<u>reht</u>·tah ahl·<u>leen</u>·gwee·neh
– a facial	– **la pulizia del viso** lah poo·<u>lee</u>·tsee·ah dehl <u>vee</u>·soh

– a manicure/ pedicure	**– un manicure/pedicure** oon mah·nee·koor·eh/peh·dee·koor·eh
– a massage	**– un massaggio** oon mahs·sah·djoh
Do you have…?	**Fate…?** fah·teh…
– acupuncture	**– l'agopuntura** lah·goh·poon·too·rah
– aromatherapy	**– l'aromaterapia** lah·roh·mah·teh·rah·pee·ah
– oxygen treatment	**– l'ossigeno terapia** lohs·see·jeh·noh teh·rah·pee·ah
Do you have a sauna?	**C'è la sauna?** cheh lah sah·ow·nah

Italy is well-known for its **stazioni termale** (spas), which can be found throughout the country. Many of these spas are located near thermal springs and offer medicinal treatments. Some are day spas and others are hotel spas, which may offer weekend packages. Tipping is optional, as service is usually included.

Hair Salon

I'd like…	**Vorrei…** vohr·ray…
– an appointment for *today/ tomorrow*	**– un appuntamento per *oggi/domani*** oon ahp·poon·tah·mehn·toh pehr *oh·djee/doh·mah·nee*
– some *color/ highlights*	**– fare *il colore/i colpi di sole*** fah·reh *eel koh·loh·reh/ee kohl·pee dee soh·leh*
– my hair *styled/ blow-dried*	**– fare la piega/asciugare** fah·reh lah pyeh·gah/ah·shoo·gah·reh
– a haircut	**– fare il taglio** fah·reh eel tah·llyoh
– a trim	**– dare una spuntatina** dah·reh oo·nah spoon·tah·tee·nah
Not too short.	**Non troppo corti.** nohn trohp·poh kohr·tee
Shorter here.	**Più corti qui.** pyoo kohr·tee kwee

Sales Help

When do you open/close?	**Quando *aprite/chiudete*?** kwahn·doh ah·*pree*·teh/kyoo·*deh*·teh
Where is/Where are…?	**Dov'è/Dove sono…?** doh·*veh*/*doh*·veh *soh*·noh…
– the cashier	**– la cassa** lah *kahs*·sah
– the elevator [lift]	**– l'ascensore** lah·shehn·*soh*·reh
– the fitting room	**– il camerino** eel kah·meh·*ree*·noh
– the store directory	**– la piantina del negozio** lah pyahn·*tee*·nah dehl neh·*goh*·tsyoh
– the escalators	**– le scale mobili** leh *skah*·leh *moh*·bee·lee
Can you help me?	**Può aiutarmi?** pwoh ah·yoo·*tahr*·mee
I'm just looking.	**Sto solo guardando.** stoh *soh*·loh gwahr·*dahn*·doh
I'm being helped.	**Mi stanno servendo.** mee *stahn*·noh sehr·*vehn*·doh
Do you have…?	**Avete…?** ah·*veh*·teh…
Can you show me…?	**Può mostrarmi…?** pwoh moh·*strahr*·mee
Can you *ship it/wrap it*?	**Può *spedirlo/incartarlo*?** pwoh speh·*deer*·loh/een·kahr·*tahr*·loh
How much?	**Quant'è?** kwahn·*teh*
That's all.	**Basta così.** *bah*·stah koh·*zee*

▶ For clothing items, see page 133.

▶ For food items, see page 90.

▶ For souvenirs, see page 131.

You May Hear...

Posso aiutarla? pohs·soh ah·yoo·tahr lah — Can I help you?

Un momento. oon moh·mehn·toh — One moment.

Che cosa desidera? keh koh·zah deh·zee·deh·rah — What would you like?

Altro? ahl·troh — Anything else?

You May See...

APERTO	open
CHIUSO	closed
ENTRATA	entrance
CAMERINO	fitting room
CASSA	cashier
SOLO CONTANTI	cash only
SI ACCETTANO CARTE DI CREDITO	credit cards accepted
ORARIO D'APERTURA	business hours
USCITA	exit

Preferences

I'd like something... **Vorrei qualcosa...** vohr·ray kwahl·koh·zah...

– cheap/expensive — **di più *economico/caro*** dee pyoo eh·koh·noh·mee·koh/kah·roh

– larger/smaller — **di più *grande/piccolo*** dee pyoo grahn·deh/peek·koh·loh

– from this region — **di tipico di questa zona** dee tee·pee·koh dee kweh·stah dzoh·nah

Around…euro.	**Intorno ai…euro.** een·<u>tohr</u>·noh <u>ah</u>·ee…<u>eh</u>·oo·roh
Is it real?	**È vero?** eh <u>veh</u>·roh
Can you show me…?	**Mi fa vedere…?** mee fah veh·<u>deh</u>·reh

Decisions

That's not quite what I want.	**Non è proprio quello che volevo.** nohn eh <u>proh</u>·pryoh <u>kwehl</u>·loh keh voh·<u>leh</u>·voh
No, I don't like it.	**No, non mi piace.** noh nohn mee <u>pyah</u>·cheh
It's too expensive.	**È troppo caro.** eh <u>trohp</u>·poh <u>kah</u>·roh
I have to think about it.	**Devo pensarci.** <u>deh</u>·voh pehn·<u>sahr</u>·chee
I'll take it.	**Lo prendo.** loh <u>prehn</u>·doh

Bargaining

That's too much.	**È troppo.** eh <u>trohp</u>·poh
I'll give you…	**Le posso dare…** leh <u>pohs</u>·soh <u>dah</u>·reh…
I have only…euro.	**Ho solo…euro.** oh <u>soh</u>·loh…<u>eh</u>·oo·roh
Is that your best price?	**È il prezzo migliore che può farmi?** eh eel <u>preh</u>·tsoh mee·<u>llyoh</u>·reh keh pwoh <u>fahr</u>·mee
Can you give me a discount?	**Mi fa un po' di sconto?** mee fah oon poh dee <u>skohn</u>·toh

▶ For numbers, see page 177.

Paying ─────────────

How much?	**Quant'è?** kwahn·<u>teh</u>
I'll pay...	**Pago...** <u>pah</u>·goh...
– in cash	– **in contanti** een kohn·<u>tahn</u>·tee
– by credit card	– **con carta di credito** kohn <u>kahr</u>·tah dee <u>kreh</u>·dee·toh
– by travelers check [cheque]	– **con un travel cheque** kohn oon <u>trah</u>·vehl chehk
Can I use...?	**Posso usare...?** <u>pohs</u>·soh oo·<u>zah</u>·reh...
– this ATM/debit card	– **questo bancomat** <u>kweh</u>·stoh <u>bahn</u>·koh·maht
– this credit card	– **questa carta di credito** <u>kweh</u>·stah <u>kahr</u>·tah dee <u>kreh</u>·dee·toh
– this gift card	– **questo buono** <u>kweh</u>·stoh <u>bwoh</u>·noh
– this prepaid card	– **questa carta prepagata** <u>kweh</u>·stah <u>kahr</u>·tah preh·pah·<u>gah</u>·tah
How do I use this machine?	**Come si usa questa macchina?** <u>koh</u>·meh see <u>oo</u>·zah <u>kweh</u>·stah <u>mahk</u>·kee·nah
How much is left on the card?	**Quanto credito c'è sulla carta?** <u>kwahn</u>·toh <u>kreh</u>·dee·toh cheh <u>sool</u>·lah <u>kahr</u>·tah
A receipt, please.	**Una ricevuta, per favore.** <u>oo</u>·nah ree·cheh·<u>voo</u>·tah pehr fah·<u>voh</u>·reh

Cash is still the most widely used and preferred method of payment, followed by **bancomat** (ATM cards). Credit cards are widely accepted, especially for larger purchases. Traveler's checks are accepted at most establishments.

Come preferisce pagare? <u>koh</u>·meh preh·feh·<u>ree</u>·sheh pah·<u>gah</u>·reh

How are you paying?

La sua carta di credito è stata rifiutata. lah <u>soo</u>·ah <u>kahr</u>·tah dee <u>kreh</u>·dee·toh eh <u>stah</u>·tah ree·fyoo·<u>tah</u>·tah

Your credit card has been declined.

Un documento, per favore. oon doh·koo·<u>mehn</u>·toh pehr fah·<u>voh</u>·reh

ID, please.

Non accettiamo carte di credito. nohn ah·cheht·<u>tyah</u>·moh <u>kahr</u>·teh dee <u>kreh</u>·dee·toh

We don't accept credit cards.

Solo contanti, per favore. <u>soh</u>·loh kohn·<u>tahn</u>·tee pehr fah·<u>voh</u>·reh

Cash only, please.

Non ha *spiccioli/banconote più piccole*? nohn ah *<u>spee</u>·chyoh·lee/bahn·koh·<u>noh</u>·teh pyoo <u>peek</u>·koh·leh*

Do you have *change/small bills [notes]*?

Grazie. grah·tsyeh

Thank you.

Buona giornata! <u>bwoh</u>·nah jyohr·<u>nah</u>·tah

Have a nice day!

Complaints

This is broken.	**È rotto♂/rotta♀.** eh roht·<u>toh</u>♂/roh·<u>tah</u>♀
I bought it yesterday.	**L'ho comprato♂/comprata♀ ieri.** loh kohm·prah·<u>toh</u>♂/kohm·prah·<u>tah</u>♀ <u>yeh</u>·ree
I'd like...	**Vorrei...** vohr·<u>ray</u>...
– to exchange this	**– cambiarlo♂/cambiarla♀** kahm·<u>byahr</u>·loh♂/kahm·<u>byahr</u>·lah♀
– a refund	**– un rimborso** oon reem·<u>bohr</u>·soh
– to see the manager	**– parlare con il responsabile** pahr·<u>lah</u>·reh kohn eel reh·spohn·<u>sah</u>·bee·leh

Souvenirs

blown glass	**il vetro soffiato** eel <u>veh</u>·troh sohf·<u>fyah</u>·toh
bottle of wine	**la bottiglia di vino** lah boht·<u>tee</u>·llyah dee <u>vee</u>·noh
box of chocolates	**la scatola di cioccolatini** lah <u>skah</u>·toh·lah dee chyohk·koh·lah·<u>tee</u>·nee
wood carvings	**il legno intagliato** eel <u>leh</u>·nyoh een·tah·<u>llyah</u>·toh
crystal	**il cristallo** eel kree·<u>stahl</u>·loh
doll	**la bambola** lah <u>bahm</u>·boh·lah
kcy ring	**il portachiavi** eel pohr·tah·<u>kyah</u>·vee
lace	**il pizzo** eel <u>pee</u>·tsoh
postcard	**la cartolina** lah kahr·toh·<u>lee</u>·nah
pottery	**la ceramica** lah cheh·<u>rah</u>·mee·kah
T-shirt	**la maglietta** lah mah·<u>llyeht</u>·tah
toy	**il giocattolo** eel jyoh·<u>kaht</u>·toh·loh
Can I see…?	**Posso vedere…?** <u>pohs</u>·soh veh·<u>deh</u>·reh…
It's in the *window/ display case.*	**È *in vetrina/nella vetrinetta.*** eh *een veh·<u>tree</u>·nah/<u>nehl</u>·lah veh·tree·<u>neht</u>·tah*
I'd like…	**Vorrei…** vohr·<u>ray</u>…
– a battery	– **una batteria** <u>oo</u>·nah baht·teh·<u>ree</u>·ah
– a bracelet	– **un braccialetto** oon brah·chyah·<u>leht</u>·toh
– a brooch	– **una spilla** <u>oo</u>·nah <u>speel</u>·lah
– a clock	– **un orologio** oo·noh·roh·<u>loh</u>·jyoh
– earrings	– **un paio di orecchini** oon <u>pah</u>·yoh dee oh·rehk·<u>kee</u>·nee
– a necklace	– **una collana** <u>oo</u>·nah kohl·<u>lah</u>·nah
– a ring	– **un anello** oo·nah·<u>nehl</u>·loh
– a watch	– **un orologio** oo·noh·roh·<u>loh</u>·jyoh

I'd like…	**Lo**♂/**La**♀ **vorrei…** loh♂/lah♀ vohr·ray…
– copper	**– di rame** dee rah·meh
– crystal	**– in cristallo** een kree·stahl·loh
– diamonds	**– di diamanti** dee dyah·mahn·tee
– *white/yellow* gold	**– d'oro *bianco/giallo*** doh·roh *byahn*·koh/*jyahl*·loh
– pearls	**– di perle** dee pehr·leh
– pewter	**– di peltro** dee pehl·troh
– platinum	**– di platino** dee plah·tee·noh
– sterling silver	**– d'argento** dahr·jehn·toh
Is this real?	**È vero?** eh veh·roh
Can you engrave it?	**Potete fare un'incisione?** poh·teh·teh fah·reh oo·neen·chee·zyoh·neh

Italy offers an endless variety of handicrafts, from mouth-blown Murano glassware and delicate Capodimonte porcelain creations, to world-renowned fashion, antiques and of course gastronomic specialties. Traditional souvenirs are usually more expensive at souvenir shops. Local markets and small shops are great places to find unique souvenirs.

Antiques

How old is it?	**Di quando è?** dee kwahn·doh eh
Do you have anything from the…period?	**Avete qualcosa del periodo…?** ah·veh·teh kwahl·koh·zah dehl peh·ryoh·doh…
Do I have to fill out any forms?	**Devo riempire un modulo?** deh·voh ree·ehm·pee·reh oon moh·doo·loh
Is there a certificate of authenticity?	**Ha il certificato di autenticità?** ah eel chehr·tee·fee·kah·toh dee ow·tehn·tee·chee·tah

Clothing

I'd like…	**Vorrei…** vohr·<u>ray</u>…
Can I try this on?	**Posso provarlo?** <u>pohs</u>·soh proh·<u>vahr</u>·loh
It doesn't fit.	**Non mi va bene.** nohn mee vah <u>beh</u>·neh
It's too…	**È troppo…** eh <u>trohp</u>·poh…
– big/small	**– grande/piccolo** <u>grahn</u>·deh/<u>peek</u>·koh·loh
– short/long	**– corto/lungo** <u>kohr</u>·toh/<u>loon</u>·goh
– tight/loose	**– stretto/largo** <u>streht</u>·toh/<u>lahr</u>·goh
Do you have this in size…?	**Non c'è la taglia…?** nohn cheh lah <u>tah</u>·llyah…
Do you have this in a *bigger/smaller* size?	**Non c'è in una taglia più *grande/piccola*?** nohn cheh een <u>oo</u>·nah <u>tah</u>·llyah pyoo <u>grahn</u>·deh/<u>peek</u>·koh·lah

▶ For numbers, see page 177.

You May See…

UOMO	men's
DONNA	women's
BAMBINO	children's

Color

I'd like something…	**Vorrei qualcosa di…** vohr·<u>ray</u> kwahl·<u>koh</u>·zah dee…
– beige	– **beige** beyj
– black	– **nero** <u>neh</u>·roh
– blue	– **blu** bloo
– brown	– **marrone** mahr·<u>roh</u>·neh
– green	– **verde** <u>vehr</u>·deh
– gray	– **grigio** <u>gree</u>·jyoh
– orange	– **arancione** ahr·ahn·<u>chyoh</u>·neh
– pink	– **rosa** <u>roh</u>·zah
– purple	– **viola** <u>vyoh</u>·lah
– red	– **rosso** <u>rohs</u>·soh
– white	– **bianco** <u>byahn</u>·koh
– yellow	– **giallo** <u>jyahl</u>·loh

Clothes and Accessories

backpack	**lo zaino** loh <u>dzah</u>·ee·noh
belt	**la cintura** lah cheen·<u>too</u>·rah
bikini	**il bikini** eel bee·<u>kee</u>·nee
blouse	**la camicia** lah kah·<u>mee</u>·chyah
bra	**il reggiseno** eel reh·djee·<u>seh</u>·noh

briefs [underpants]	**lo slip** loh sleep
coat	**il cappotto** eel kahp·<u>poht</u>·toh
dress	**il vestito da donna** eel veh·<u>stee</u>·toh dah dohn·nah
hat	**il cappello** eel kahp·<u>pehl</u>·loh
jacket	**la giacca** lah <u>jyahk</u>·kah
jeans	**i jeans** ee jeenz
pajamas	**il pigiama** eel pee·<u>jyah</u>·mah
pants [trousers]	**i pantaloni** ee pahn·tah·<u>loh</u>·nee
pantyhose [tights]	**il collant** eel kohl·<u>lant</u>
purse [handbag]	**la borsa** lah <u>bohr</u>·sah
raincoat	**l'impermeabile** leem·pehr·meh·<u>ah</u>·bee·leh
scarf	**la sciarpa** lah <u>shahr</u>·pah
shirt	**la camicia** lah kah·<u>mee</u>·chyah
shorts	**i pantaloncini** ee pahn·tah·lohn·<u>chee</u>·nee
skirt	**la gonna** lah <u>gohn</u>·nah
socks	**i calzini** ee kahl·<u>tsee</u>·nee
suit	**l'abito** <u>lah</u>·bee·toh
sunglasses	**gli occhiali da sole** llyee ohk·<u>kyah</u>·lee dah <u>soh</u>·leh
sweater	**il maglione** eel mah·<u>llyoh</u>·neh
sweatshirt	**la felpa** lah <u>fehl</u>·pah
swimsuit	**il costume da bagno** eel koh·<u>stoo</u>·meh dah <u>bah</u>·nyoh
T-shirt	**la maglietta** lah mah·<u>llyeht</u>·tah
tie	**la cravatta** lah krah·<u>vaht</u>·tah
underwear	**la biancheria intima** lah byahn·keh·<u>ree</u>·ah <u>een</u>·tee·mah

Fabric

I'd like…	**Lo♂/La♀ vorrei di…** loh vohr·ray dee…
– cotton	**– cotone** koh·toh·neh
– denim	**– jeans** jeenz
– lace	**– pizzo** pee·tsoh
– leather	**– pelle** pehl·leh
– linen	**– lino** lee·noh
– silk	**– seta** seh·tah
– wool	**– lana** lah·nah
Is it machine washable?	**Si può lavare in lavatrice?** see pwoh lah·vah·reh een lah·vah·tree·cheh

Shoes

I'd like a pair of…	**Vorrei un paio di…** vohr·ray oon pah·yoh dee…
– boots	**– stivali** stee·vah·lee
– loafers	**– mocassini** moh·kahs·see·nee
– sandals	**– sandali** sahn·dah·lee
– shoes	**– scarpe** skahr·peh
– slippers	**– le ciabatte** leh chah·baht·teh
– sneakers	**– scarpe da tennis** skahr·peh dah tehn·nees
In size…	**Numero…** noo·meh·roh…

▶For numbers, see page 177.

Sizes

small (S)	**piccola/S** pee·koh·lah/ehs·seh
medium (M)	**media/M** meh·dyah/ehm·meh
large (L)	**grande/L** grahn·deh/ehl·leh
extra large (XL)	**extra large/XL** ehk·strah lahrj/ehks·ehl
plus size	**taglia forte** tah·llyah fohr·teh

Do you sell English-language newspapers?	**Avete qualche giornale in inglese?** ah·<u>veh</u>·teh <u>kwahl</u>·keh jyohr·<u>nah</u>·leh een een·<u>gleh</u>·zeh
I'd like…	**Vorrei…** vohr·<u>ray</u>…
– candy [sweets]	**– delle caramelle** <u>dehl</u>·leh kah·rah·<u>mehl</u>·leh
– chewing gum	**– della gomma da masticare** <u>dehl</u>·lah <u>gohm</u>·mah dah mah·stee·<u>kah</u>·reh
– a chocolate bar	**– del cioccolato** dehl chyohk·koh·<u>lah</u>·toh
– a cigar	**– un sigaro** oon <u>see</u>·gah·roh
– a *pack/carton* of cigarettes	**– *un pacchetto/una stecca* di sigarette** *oon pahk·<u>keht</u>·toh/<u>oo</u>·nah <u>stehk</u>·kah dee see·gah·<u>reht</u>·teh*
– a lighter	**– un accendino** oon·ah·chehn·<u>dee</u>·noh
– a magazine	**– una rivista** <u>oo</u>·nah ree·<u>vee</u>·stah
– matches	**– dei fiammiferi** day fyahm·<u>mee</u>·feh·ree
– a newspaper	**– un giornale** oon jyohr·<u>nah</u>·leh
– a pen	**– una penna** <u>oo</u>·nah <u>pehn</u>·nah
– a postcard	**– una cartolina** <u>oo</u>·nah kahr·toh·<u>lee</u>·nah
– a (road) map of…	**– una cartina (stradale) di…** <u>oo</u>·nah kahr·<u>tee</u>·nah (strah·<u>dah</u>·lee) dee…
– stamps	**– dei francobolli** day frahn·koh·<u>bohl</u>·lee

English-language newspapers, magazines and books are available at most newsstands, especially at train stations and airports.

Smoking is not allowed in any public facility (banks, offices, bars, cafes, restaurants, buses, trains, etc.). Be aware that no-smoking signs are not posted but you will incur a high fine if caught smoking in any public indoor area.

Photography

I'd like a/an… camera.	**Vorrei una macchina fotografica…** vohr·<u>ray</u> <u>oo</u>·nah <u>mahk</u>·kee·nah foh·toh·<u>grah</u>·fee·kah…
– automatic	– **automatica** ow·toh·<u>mah</u>·tee·kah
– digital	– **digitale** dee·jee·<u>tah</u>·leh
– disposable	– **usa e getta** <u>oo</u>·zah eh <u>jeht</u>·tah
I'd like…	**Vorrei…** vohr·<u>ray</u>…
– a battery	– **una batteria** <u>oo</u>·nah baht·teh·<u>ree</u>·ah
– digital prints	– **far stampare delle foto digitali** fahr stahm·<u>pah</u>·reh <u>dehl</u>·leh <u>foh</u>·toh dee·jee·<u>tah</u>·lee
– a memory card	– **una scheda memoria** <u>oo</u>·nah <u>skeh</u>·dah meh·<u>moh</u>·ryah
Can I print digital photos here?	**Posso stampare foto digitali?** <u>pohs</u>·soh stahm·<u>pah</u>·reh <u>foh</u>·toh dee·jee·<u>tah</u>·lee

Sports and Leisure

Essential

When's the game?	**A che ora c'è la partita?** ah keh <u>oh</u>·rah cheh lah pahr·<u>tee</u>·tah
Where's…?	**Dov'è…?** doh·<u>veh</u>…
– the beach	– **la spiaggia** lah <u>spyah</u>·djah
– the park	– **il parco** eel <u>pahr</u>·koh
– the pool	– **la piscina** lah pee·<u>shee</u>·nah
Is it safe to swim here?	**Si può nuotare?** see pwoh nwoh·<u>tah</u>·reh
Can I rent [hire] golf clubs?	**Posso noleggiare delle mazze?** <u>pohs</u>·soh noh·leh·<u>djah</u>·reh <u>dehl</u>·leh <u>mah</u>·tseh

How much per hour?	**Qual è la tariffa per un'ora?** kwah·leh lah tah·<u>reef</u>·fah pehr oo·<u>noh</u>·rah
How far is it to…?	**Quanto dista a…?** kwahn·toh <u>dee</u>·stah ah…
Can you show me on the map?	**Può indicarmelo sulla cartina?** pwoh een·dee·<u>kahr</u>·meh·loh <u>sool</u>·lah kahr·<u>tee</u>·nah

Spectator Sports

When's…?	**A che ora c'è…?** ah keh <u>oh</u>·rah cheh…
– the baseball game	– **la partita di baseball** lah pahr·<u>tee</u>·tah dee <u>bays</u>·bahl
– the basketball game	– **la partita di basket** lah pahr·<u>tee</u>·tah dee <u>bahs</u>·keht
– the boxing match	– **l'incontro di boxe** leen·<u>kohn</u>·troh dee <u>boh</u>·kseh
– the cycling race	– **la gara di ciclismo** lah <u>gah</u>·rah dee chee·<u>kleez</u>·moh
– the golf game	– **la partita di golf** lah pahr·<u>tee</u>·tah dee gohlf
– the soccer [football] game	– **la partita di calcio** lah pahr·<u>tee</u>·tah dee <u>kahl</u>·chyoh
– the tennis match	– **la partita di tennis** lah pahr·<u>tee</u>·tah dee <u>tehn</u>·nees
– the volleyball game	– **la partita di pallavolo** lah pahr·<u>tee</u>·tah dee pahl·lah·<u>voh</u>·loh
Who's playing?	**Chi gioca?** kee <u>jyoh</u>·kah
Where's the *racetrack/stadium*?	**Dov'è *il circuito/lo stadio*?** doh·veh *eel cheer·<u>kwee</u>·toh/loh <u>stah</u>·dyoh*
Where can I place a bet?	**Dove si fanno le scommesse?** <u>doh</u>·veh see <u>fahn</u>·noh leh skohm·<u>mehs</u>·seh

▶ For ticketing, see page 19.

139

i Il calcio (soccer) is Italy's most popular year-round sport. Skiing and snowboarding are favorite winter pastimes for Italians. During the summer, sailing, windsurfing, hiking, tennis, scuba-diving, hang-gliding—especially on Lake Garda—and swimming are enjoyed.

Participating

Where is/Where are…?	**Dov'è/Dove sono…?** doh·<u>veh</u>/<u>doh</u>·veh <u>soh</u>·noh…
– the golf course	**– il campo da golf** eel <u>kahm</u>·poh dah gohlf
– the gym	**– la palestra** lah pah·<u>leh</u>·strah
– the park	**– il parco** eel <u>pahr</u>·koh
– the tennis courts	**– i campi da tennis** ee <u>kahm</u>·pee dah <u>teh</u>·nees
How much…?	**Quant'è la tariffa per…?** kwahn·<u>teh</u> lah tah·<u>reef</u>·fah pehr…
– per day	**– un giorno** oon <u>jyohr</u>·noh
– per hour	**– un'ora** oon·<u>oh</u>·rah
– per game	**– una partita** <u>oo</u>·nah pahr·<u>tee</u>·tah
Can I rent [hire]…	**Posso noleggiare…** <u>pohs</u>·soh noh·leh·<u>djah</u>·reh…
– golf clubs	**– delle mazze** <u>dehl</u>·leh <u>mah</u>·tseh

| – equipment | **– l'attrezzatura** laht·treh·tsah·<u>too</u>·rah |
| – a racket | **– una racchetta** <u>oo</u>·nah rahk·<u>keht</u>·tah |

At the Beach/Pool

Where's the *beach/pool*?	**Dov'è la *spiaggia/piscina*?** doh·<u>veh</u> lah *<u>spyah</u>·djah/pee·<u>shee</u>·nah*
Is there…?	**C'è…?** cheh…
– a kiddie pool	**– una piscina per bambini** <u>oo</u>·nah pee·<u>shee</u>·nah pehr bahm·<u>bee</u>·nee
– a indoor/outdoor pool	**– una piscina *interna/esterna*** <u>oo</u>·nah pee·<u>shee</u>·nah *een·<u>tehr</u>·nah/eh·<u>stehr</u>·nah*
– a lifeguard	**– il bagnino** eel bah·<u>nyee</u>·noh
Is it safe to *swim/dive*?	**Si può *nuotare/tuffarsi*?** see pwoh *nwoh·<u>tah</u>·reh/toof·<u>fahr</u>·see*
Is it safe for children?	**È per bambini?** eh pehr bahm·<u>bee</u>·nee

▶ For travel with children, see page 152.

I'd like to rent [hire]…	**Vorrei noleggiare…** vohr·<u>ray</u> noh·leh·<u>djah</u>·reh
– a deck chair	**– una sedia a sdraio** <u>oo</u>·nah <u>seh</u>·dyah ah <u>sdrah</u>·yoh
– diving equipment	**– l'attrezzatura subacquea** laht·treh·tsah·<u>too</u>·rah soo·<u>bah</u>·kweh·ah
– a jet ski	**– un acquascooter** oon <u>ah</u>·kwah·<u>skoo</u>·tehr
– a motorboat	**– un motoscafo** oon moh·toh·<u>skah</u>·foh
– a rowboat	**– una barca a remi** <u>oo</u>·nah <u>bahr</u>·kah ah <u>reh</u>·mee
– snorkeling equipment	**– una maschera e il boccaglio** <u>oo</u>·nah <u>mah</u>·skeh·rah eh eel bohk·<u>kah</u>·llyoh

I'd like to rent [hire]…	**Vorrei noleggiare…** vohr·<u>ray</u> noh·leh·djah·reh
– a surfboard	**– una tavola da surf** <u>oo</u>·nah <u>tah</u>·voh·lah dah soorf
– a towel	**– un asciugamano** oon ah·shyoo·gah·<u>mah</u>·noh
– an umbrella	**– un ombrellone** oon ohm·brehl·<u>loh</u>·neh
– water skis	**– sci nautici** shee <u>now</u>·tee·chee
– a windsurfer	**– un windsurf** oon <u>weend</u>·soorf
For…hours.	**Per…ore.** pehr…<u>oh</u>·reh

With 7,600 kilometers (4,722 miles) of coastline, Italy has beaches to suit all tastes and budgets. From exclusive Ligurian and Sardinian beaches to popular Versilian and Adriatic spots, the seaside is a favorite holiday destination for Italians. Privately managed beaches are usually well-kept and offer a variety of services for a daily fee.

Winter Sports

A lift pass for *a day/five days*, please.	**Un lift pass per *un giorno/cinque giorni*, per favore.** oon leeft pahs pehr *oon <u>jyohr</u>·noh/ <u>cheen</u>·kweh <u>jyohr</u>·nee* pehr fah·<u>voh</u>·reh
I'd like to rent [hire]…	**Vorrei noleggiare…** vohr·<u>ray</u> noh·leh·djah·reh…
– boots	**– un paio di stivali** oon <u>pah</u>·yoh dee stee·<u>vah</u>·lee
– a helmet	**– un casco** oon <u>kah</u>·skoh
– poles	**– un paio di racchette da sci** oon <u>pah</u>·yoh dee rahk·<u>keht</u>·teh dah shee
– skis	**– un paio di sci** oon <u>pah</u>·yoh dee shee
– a snowboard	**– uno snowboard** <u>oo</u>·noh <u>snoh</u>·bohrd
– snowshoes	**– le scarpe da neve** lah <u>skahr</u>·peh dah <u>neh</u>·veh

These are too *big/small.*	**Sono troppo *grandi/piccoli.*** <u>soh</u>·noh <u>trohp</u>·poh *grahn·dee/peek·koh·lee*
Are there lessons?	**Si possono prendere lezioni?** see <u>pohs</u>·soh·noh <u>prehn</u>·deh·reh leh·<u>tsyoh</u>·nee
I'm a beginner.	**Sono principiante.** <u>soh</u>·noh preen·chee·<u>pyahn</u>·teh
I'm experienced.	**Sono esperto ♂ /esperta ♀ .** <u>soh</u>·noh eh·<u>spehr</u>·toh ♂ /eh·<u>spehr</u>·tah ♀
A trail [piste] map, please.	**Una cartina delle piste, per favore.** <u>oo</u>·nah kahr·<u>tee</u>·nah <u>dehl</u>·leh <u>pee</u>·steh pehr fah·<u>voh</u>·reh

You May See...

SKI LIFT	drag lift
FUNIVIA	cable car
SEGGIOVIA	chair lift
PRINCIPIANTE	novice
INTERMEDIO	intermediate
ESPERTO	expert
PISTA CHIUSA	trail [piste] closed

In the Countryside

A map…, please.	**Una cartina…, per favore.** <u>oo</u>·nah kahr·<u>tee</u>·nah…pehr fah·<u>voh</u>·reh
– of this region	– **della regione** <u>dehl</u>·lah reh·<u>jyoh</u>·neh
– of the walking routes	– **dei sentieri pedonali** day sehn·<u>tyeh</u>·ree peh·doh·<u>nah</u>·lee
– of the bike routes	– **delle piste ciclabili** <u>dehl</u>·leh <u>pee</u>·steh chee·<u>klah</u>·bee·lee
– of the trails	– **dei sentieri** day sehn·<u>tyeh</u>·ree

143

Is it…?	**È…?** eh…
– easy	– **facile** <u>fah</u>·chee·leh
– difficult	– **difficile** deef·<u>fee</u>·chee·leh
– far	– **lontano** lohn·<u>tah</u>·noh
– steep	– **ripido** <u>ree</u>·pee·doh
How far is it to…?	**Quanto dista a…?** <u>kwahn</u>·toh <u>dee</u>·stah ah…
Can you show me on the map?	**Può indicarmelo sulla cartina?** pwoh een·dee·<u>kahr</u>·meh·loh <u>sool</u>·lah kahr·<u>tee</u>·nah
I'm lost.	**Mi sono perso♂/persa♀.** mee <u>soh</u>·noh <u>pehr</u>·soh♂/<u>pehr</u>·sah♀
Where's…?	**Dov'è…?** doh·<u>veh</u>…
– the bridge	– **il ponte** eel <u>pohn</u>·teh
– the cave	– **la grotta** lah <u>groht</u>·tah
– the farm	– **la fattoria** lah faht·toh·<u>ree</u>·ah
– the field	– **il campo** eel <u>kahm</u>·poh
– the forest	– **la foresta** lah foh·<u>reh</u>·stah
– the hill	– **la collina** lah kohl·<u>lee</u>·nah
– the lake	– **il lago** eel <u>lah</u>·goh
– the mountain	– **la montagna** lah mohn·<u>tah</u>·nyah
– the nature preserve	– **la riserva naturale** lah ree·<u>sehr</u>·vah nah·too·<u>rah</u>·leh
– the overlook [viewpoint]	– **il belvedere** eel behl·veh·<u>deh</u>·reh
– the park	– **il parco** eel <u>pahr</u>·koh
– the path	– **il sentiero** eel sehn·<u>tyeh</u>·roh
– the peak	– **il picco** eel <u>peek</u>·koh
– the picnic area	– **l'area picnic** <u>lah</u>·reh·ah <u>peek</u>·neek
– the pond	– **lo stagno** loh <u>stah</u>·nyoh

– the river	– **il fiume** eel <u>fyoo</u>·meh
– the sea	– **il mare** eel <u>mah</u>·reh
– the (thermal) spring	– **la sorgente (termale)** lah sohr·<u>jehn</u>·teh (tehr·<u>mah</u>·leh)
– the stream	– **il ruscello** eel roo·<u>shehl</u>·loh
– the valley	– **la valle** lah <u>vahl</u>·leh
– the vineyard	– **il vigneto** eel vee·<u>nyeh</u>·toh
– the waterfall	– **la cascata** lah kah·<u>skah</u>·tah

Culture and Nightlife

Essential

What's there to do at night?	**Cosa si fa di sera?** <u>koh</u>·zah see fah dee <u>seh</u>·rah
Do you have a program of events?	**Mi può dare un calendario degli eventi?** mee pwoh <u>dah</u>·reh oon kah·lehn·<u>dah</u>·ryoh <u>deh</u>·llyee eh·<u>vehn</u>·tee
What's playing tonight?	**Cosa c'è in programma stasera?** <u>koh</u>·zah cheh een proh·<u>grahm</u>·mah stah·<u>seh</u>·rah
Where's...?	**Dov'è...?** doh·<u>veh</u>...
– the downtown area	– **il centro** eel <u>chehn</u>·troh
– the bar	– **il bar** eel bahr
– the dance club	– **la discoteca** lah dee·skoh·<u>teh</u>·kah
Is there a cover charge?	**C'è un costo aggiuntivo?** cheh oon <u>koh</u>·stoh ah·djoon·<u>tee</u>·voh

Entertainment

Can you recommend…?	**Può consigliarmi…?** pwoh kohn·see·<u>llyahr</u>·mee…
– a concert	**– un concerto** oon kohn·<u>chehr</u>·toh
– a movie	**– un film** oon feelm
– an opera	**– un'opera** oo·<u>noh</u>·peh·rah
– a play	**– una rappresentazione teatrale** <u>oo</u>·nah rahp·preh·zehn·tah·<u>tsyoh</u>·neh teh·ah·<u>trah</u>·leh
When does it start/end?	**Quando *inizia/finisce*?** <u>kwahn</u>·doh ee·<u>nee</u>·tsyah/fee·<u>nee</u>·sheh
What's the dress code?	**Come ci si deve vestire?** <u>koh</u>·meh chee see <u>deh</u>·veh veh·<u>stee</u>·reh
I like…	**Mi piace…** mee <u>pyah</u>·cheh…
– classical music	**– la musica classica** lah <u>moo</u>·zee·kah <u>klah</u>·see·kah
– folk music	**– la musica folk** lah <u>moo</u>·zee·kah fohlk
– jazz	**– il jazz** eel jahz
– pop music	**– la musica pop** lah <u>moo</u>·zee·kah pohp
– rap	**– il rap** eel rahp

▶For ticketing, see page 19.

A calendar of events may be found at local tourist information offices or on the venues' websites. Local events are often posted around town, so be sure to stop and read the posters. The hotel concierge is also a good source for local information.

You May Hear...

Spegnere il cellulare, per favore.
speh·nyeh·reh eel chehl·loo·lah·reh pehr
fah·voh·reh

Turn off your cell [mobile] phones, please.

Nightlife

What's there to do at night?	**Cosa si fa di sera?** koh·zah see fah dee seh·rah
Can you recommend...?	**Può consigliarmi...?** pwoh kohn·see·llyahr·mee...
– a bar	**– un bar** oon bahr
– a casino	**– un casinò** oon kah·zee·noh
– a dance club	**– una discoteca** oo·nah dee·skoh·teh·kah
– a gay club	**– un locale gay** oon loh·kah·leh gay
– a jazz club	**– un locale jazz** oon loh·kah·leh jahz
– a club with Italian music	**– un locale con musica italiana** oon loh·kah·leh kohn moo·zee·kah ee·tah·lyah·nah
Is there live music?	**C'è musica dal vivo?** cheh moo·zee·kah dahl vee·voh
How do I get there?	**Come ci si arriva?** koh·meh chee see ahr·ree·vah
Is there a cover charge?	**C'è un costo aggiuntivo?** cheh oon koh·stoh ah·djoon·tee·voh
Let's go dancing.	**Andiamo a ballare.** ahn·dyah·moh ah bahl·lah·reh

▼ Special Needs

Essential

I'm here on business.	**Sono qui per lavoro.** <u>soh</u>·noh kwee pehr lah·<u>voh</u>·roh
Here's my business card.	**Ecco il mio biglietto da visita.** <u>ehk</u>·koh eel <u>mee</u>·oh bee·<u>llyeht</u>·toh dah <u>vee</u>·zee·tah
Can I have your card?	**Mi può dare il suo biglietto da visita?** mee pwoh <u>dah</u>·reh eel <u>soo</u>·oh bee·<u>llyeht</u>·toh dah <u>vee</u>·zee·tah
I have a meeting with...	**Ho una riunione con...** oh <u>oo</u>·nah ryoo·<u>nyoh</u>·neh kohn...
Where's...?	**Dov'è...?** doh·<u>veh</u>...
– the business center	**– il centro business** eel <u>chehn</u>·troh <u>bees</u>·nehs
– the convention hall	**– la sala congressi** lah <u>sah</u>·lah kohn·<u>grehs</u>·see
– the meeting room	**– la sala meeting** lah <u>sah</u>·lah <u>mee</u>·teeng

---

Buongiorno (good morning) or **buonasera** (good afternoon/ evening) are suitable greetings in business situations, and are often accompanied by a handshake. **Piacere** (pleased to meet you) is a polite response at introductions. When saying goodbye to business acquaintances, it is polite to use the formal **arrivederla**.

Business Communication

I'm here for...	**Sono qui per...** <u>soh</u>·noh kwee pehr...
– a seminar	**– un seminario** oon seh·mee·<u>nah</u>·ryoh
– a conference	**– una conferenza** <u>oo</u>·nah kohn·feh·<u>rehn</u>·tsah
– a meeting	**– una riunione** <u>oo</u>·nah ryoo·<u>nyoh</u>·neh

My name is…	**Mi chiamo…** mee <u>kyah</u>·moh…
May I introduce my colleague…	**Le presento il mio collega♂/la mia collega♀…** leh preh·<u>zehn</u>·toh eel <u>mee</u>·oh kohl·<u>leh</u>·gah♂/lah <u>mee</u>·ah kohl·<u>leh</u>·gah♀…
I have *a meeting/an appointment* with…	**Ho *una riunione/un appuntamento* con…** oh <u>oo</u>·nah ryoo·<u>nyoh</u>·neh/oon ahp·<u>poon</u>·tah·<u>mehn</u>·toh kohn…
I'm sorry I'm late.	**Scusi il ritardo.** <u>skoo</u>·see eel ree·<u>tahr</u>·doh
I need an interpreter.	**Mi serve un interprete.** mee <u>sehr</u>·veh oon een·<u>tehr</u>·preh·teh
You can reach me at the…Hotel.	**Sono raggiungibile all'hotel…** <u>soh</u>·noh rah·djoon·<u>jee</u>·bee·leh ahl·loh·<u>tehl</u>…
I'm here until…	**Sono qui fino a…** <u>soh</u>·noh kwee <u>fee</u>·noh ah…

I need to…	**Ho bisogno di…** oh bee·<u>soh</u>·nyoh dee…
– make a call	**– fare una telefonata** <u>fah</u>·reh <u>oo</u>·nah teh·leh·foh·<u>nah</u>·tah
– make a photocopy	**– fare una fotocopia** <u>fah</u>·reh <u>oo</u>·nah foh·toh·<u>koh</u>·pyah
– send an e-mail	**– inviare un'e-mail** een·<u>vyah</u>·reh oon <u>ee</u>·mayl
– send a fax	**– inviare un fax** een·<u>vyah</u>·reh oon fahks
– send a package (overnight)	**– inviare un pacco (da un giorno all'altro)** een·<u>vyah</u>·reh oon <u>pahk</u>·koh (dah oon <u>jyohr</u>·noh ahl·<u>lahl</u>·troh)
It was a pleasure to meet you.	**È stato un piacere.** eh <u>stah</u>·toh oon pyah·<u>cheh</u>·reh

▶ For internet and communications, see page 47.

You May Hear…

Ha un appuntamento? ah oon ahp·<u>poon</u>·tah·<u>mehn</u>·toh	Do you have an appointment?
Con chi? kohn kee	With whom?
Il signor ♂/La signora ♀ è in riunione. eel see·<u>nyohr</u> ♂/lah see·<u>nyoh</u>·rah ♀ eh een ryoo·<u>nyoh</u>·neh	He/She is in a meeting.
Un momento, per favore. oon moh·<u>mehn</u>·toh pehr fah·<u>voh</u>·reh	One moment, please.
Si accomodi. see ahk·<u>koh</u>·moh·dee	Have a seat.
Desidera qualcosa da bere? deh·<u>zee</u>·deh·rah kwahl·<u>koh</u>·zah dah <u>beh</u>·reh	Would you like something to drink?
Grazie per essere venuto ♂/venuta ♀. <u>grah</u>·tsyeh pehr <u>eh</u>·seh·reh veh·<u>noo</u>·toh ♂/veh·<u>noo</u>·tah ♀	Thank you for coming.

Essential

Is there a discount for kids?	**È previsto uno sconto per bambini?** eh preh·<u>vee</u>·stoh <u>oo</u>·noh <u>skohn</u>·toh pehr bahm·<u>bee</u>·nee
Can you recommend a babysitter?	**Può consigliarmi una babysitter?** pwoh kohn·see·<u>llyahr</u>·mee <u>oo</u>·nah bah·bee·<u>seet</u>·tehr
Do you have a child's *seat/highchair*?	**Avete un *seggiolino/seggiolone* per bambini?** ah·<u>veh</u>·teh oon seh·djoh·<u>lee</u>·noh/ seh·djoh·<u>loh</u>·neh pehr bahm·<u>bee</u>·nee
Where can I change the baby?	**Dove posso cambiare il bambino?** <u>doh</u>·veh <u>poh</u>·soh kahm·<u>byah</u>·reh eel bahm·<u>bee</u>·noh

Fun with Kids

Can you recommend something for kids?	**Può consigliarmi qualcosa per i bambini?** pwoh kohn·see·<u>llyahr</u>·mee kwahl·<u>koh</u>·zah pehr ee bahm·<u>bee</u>·nee
Where's…?	**Dov'è…?** doh·<u>veh</u>…
– the amusement park	**– il luna park** eel <u>loo</u>·nah pahrk
– the arcade	**– il parco videogiochi** eel <u>pahr</u>·koh <u>vee</u>·deh·oh·<u>jyoh</u>·kee
– the kiddie [paddling] pool	**– la piscina per bambini** lah pee·<u>shee</u>·nah pehr bahm·<u>bee</u>·nee
– the park	**– il parco** eel <u>pahr</u>·koh
– the playground	**– il parco giochi** eel <u>pahr</u>·koh <u>jyoh</u>·kee
– the zoo	**– lo zoo** loh dzooh

Are kids allowed?	**Si possono portare i bambini?** see <u>pohs</u>·soh·noh pohr·<u>tah</u>·reh ee bahm·<u>bee</u>·nee
Is it safe for kids?	**È per bambini?** eh pehr bahm·<u>bee</u>·nee
Is it suitable for…year olds?	**È adatto ai bambini di…anni?** eh ah·<u>daht</u>·toh <u>ah</u>·ee bahm·<u>bee</u>·nee dee…<u>ahn</u>·nee

▶For numbers, see page 177.

Che carino♂/carina♀!
keh kah·<u>ree</u>·noh♂/kah·<u>ree</u>·nah♀

How cute!

Come si chiama?
<u>koh</u>·meh see <u>kyah</u>·mah

What's his/her name?

Quanti anni ha?
<u>kwahn</u>·tee <u>ahn</u>·nee ah

How old is he/she?

Basic Needs for Kids

Do you have...?   **Avete...?** ah·<u>veh</u>·teh...

– a baby bottle   **– un biberon** oon bee·beh·<u>rohn</u>

– baby food   **– del cibo per neonati** dehl <u>chee</u>·boh pehr neh·oh·<u>nah</u>·tee

– baby wipes   **– delle salviette per neonati** <u>dehl</u>·leh sahl·<u>vyeht</u>·teh pehr neh·oh·<u>nah</u>·tee

– a car seat   **– un seggiolino per auto** oon seh·djoh·<u>lee</u>·noh pehr <u>ow</u>·toh

– a children's *menu/portion*   **– *il menù/le porzioni* per bambini** eel meh·<u>noo</u>/leh pohr·<u>tsyoh</u>·nee pehr bahm·bee·nee

▶ For dining with kids, see page 61.

– a child's *seat/ highchair*   **– un *seggiolino/seggiolone* per bambini** oon seh·djoh·<u>lee</u>·noh/seh·djoh·<u>loh</u>·neh pehr bahm·<u>bee</u>·nee

– a crib/cot   **– una culla/un lettino** <u>oo</u>·nah <u>kool</u>·lah/oon leht·<u>tee</u>·noh

– diapers [nappies]   **– dei pannolini** day pahn·noh·<u>lee</u>·nee

– formula [baby food]   **– del latte in polvere** dehl <u>laht</u>·teh een <u>pohl</u>·veh·reh

– a pacifier [soother]   **– un ciucciotto** oon chyoo·<u>chyoht</u>·toh

– a playpen   **– un box** oon bohks

– a stroller   **– un passeggino** oon pah·seh·<u>djee</u>·noh
   [pushchair]

Can I breastfeed   **Posso allattare il bambino?** <u>poh</u>·soh
the baby here?   ahl·laht·<u>tah</u>·reh eel bahm·<u>bee</u>·noh

Where can I   **Dove posso *allattare/cambiare* il bambino?**
breastfeed/change   <u>doh</u>·veh <u>poh</u>·soh *ahl·laht·<u>tah</u>·reh/*
the baby?   *kahm·<u>byah</u>·reh* eel bahm·<u>bee</u>·noh

Babysitting

Can you recommend   **Può consigliarmi una babysitter?** pwoh
a babysitter?   kohn·see·<u>llyahr</u>·mee <u>oo</u>·nah bah·bee·<u>seet</u>·tehr

What do *you/they*   **Quanto si paga?** <u>kwahn</u>·toh see <u>pah</u>·gah
charge?

I'll be back by…   **Torno per le…** <u>tohr</u>·noh pehr leh…

▶ For time, see page 179.

You can reach   **Mi potete trovare al numero…** mee
me at…   poh·<u>tay</u>·teh troh·<u>vahr</u>·eh ahl <u>noo</u>·meh·roh…

▶ For numbers, see page 177.

Health and Emergency

Can you recommend   **Può consigliarmi un pediatra?** pwoh
a pediatrician?   kohn·see·<u>llyahr</u>·mee oon peh·<u>dyah</u>·trah

My son/daughter is   **Il mio bambino/La mia bambina è**
allergic to…   **allergico♂/allergica♀ a…** eel <u>mee</u>·oh
   bahm·<u>bee</u>·noh/lah <u>mee</u>·ah bahm·<u>bee</u>·nah
   eh ahl·<u>lehr</u>·jee·koh♂/ahl·<u>lehr</u>·jee·kah♀ ah…

| My son/daughter is missing. | **Il mio bambino/La mia bambina è scomparso♂/scomparsa♀.** eel <u>mee</u>·oh bahm·<u>bee</u>·noh/lah <u>mee</u>·ah bahm·<u>bee</u>·nah eh skohm·<u>pahr</u>·soh♂/skohm·<u>pahr</u>·sah♀ |
| Have you seen a *boy/girl*? | **Ha visto** *un bambino/una bambina*? ah <u>vee</u>·stoh *oon bahm·<u>bee</u>·noh/<u>oo</u>·nah bahm·<u>bee</u>·nah* |

▶ For food items, see page 90.

▶ For health, see page 162.

▶ For police, see page 159.

For the Disabled

Essential

Is there…?	**C'è…?** cheh…
– access for the disabled	– **l'accesso ai disabili** lah·<u>cheh</u>·soh <u>ah</u>·ee dee·<u>zah</u>·bee·lee
– a wheelchair ramp	– **la rampa per le sedie a rotelle** lah <u>rahm</u>·pah pehr leh <u>seh</u>·dyeh ah roh·<u>tehl</u>·leh
– a handicapped- [disabled-] accessible restroom	– **la toilette per i disabili** lah twah·leht pehr ee dee·<u>zah</u>·bee·lee
I need…	**Mi serve…** mee <u>sehr</u>·veh…
– assistance	– **assistenza** ah·see·<u>stehn</u>·tsah
– an elevator [a lift]	– **un ascensore** oon ah·shehn·<u>soh</u>·reh
– a ground-floor room	– **una stanza al pianterreno** <u>oo</u>·nah <u>stahn</u>·tsah ahl pyahn·tehr·<u>reh</u>·noh

Getting Help

I'm...

Sono... <u>soh</u>·noh...

– disabled

– **disabile** dee·<u>zah</u>·bee·leh

– visually impaired

– **ipovedente** ee·poh·veh·<u>dehn</u>·teh

– hearing impaired/ deaf

– **audioleso/sordo** ow·dyoh·<u>leh</u>·soh/<u>sohr</u>·doh

I cannot *walk far/ use the stairs.*

Non posso *camminare tanto/fare le scale.* nohn <u>poh</u>·soh *kahm·mee·<u>nah</u>·reh tahn·toh/<u>fah</u>·reh leh <u>skah</u>·leh*

Can I bring my wheelchair?

Posso portare la sedia a rotelle? <u>poh</u>·soh pohr·<u>tah</u>·reh lah <u>seh</u>·dyah ah roh·<u>tehl</u>·leh

Are guide dogs permitted?

I cani guida sono permessi? ee <u>kah</u>·nee <u>gwee</u>·dah <u>soh</u>·noh pehr·<u>meh</u>·see

Can you help me?

Può aiutarmi? pwoh ah·yoo·<u>tahr</u>·mee

Please *open/hold* the door.

Per favore, potrebbe *aprire/tenere aperta* la porta. pehr fah·<u>voh</u>·reh poh·<u>trehb</u>·beh *ah·<u>pree</u>·reh/teh·<u>neh</u>·reh ah·<u>pehr</u>·tah* lah <u>pohr</u>·tah

▼ Resources

Emergencies

Essential

Help!	**Aiuto!** ah·<u>yoo</u>·toh
Go away!	**Se ne vada!** seh neh <u>vah</u>·dah
Stop, thief!	**Fermi, al ladro!** <u>fehr</u>·mee ahl <u>lah</u>·droh
Get a doctor!	**Un medico!** oon <u>meh</u>·dee·koh
Fire!	**Al fuoco!** ahl <u>fwoh</u>·koh
I'm lost.	**Mi sono perso ♂/persa ♀.** mee <u>soh</u>·noh <u>pehr</u>·soh ♂/<u>pehr</u>·sah ♀
Can you help me?	**Può aiutarmi?** pwoh ah·yoo·<u>tahr</u>·mee

Police

Essential

Call the police!	**Chiami la polizia!** <u>kyah</u>·mee lah poh·lee·<u>tsee</u>·ah
Where's the police station?	**Dov'è il commissariato?** doh·<u>veh</u> eel kohm·mee·sah·<u>ryah</u>·toh
There was an *accident/attack*.	**C'è *stato un incidente/stata un'aggressione*.** cheh <u>stah</u>·toh oon een·chee·<u>dehn</u>·teh/<u>stah</u>·tah oo·nahg·grehs·<u>syoh</u>·neh
My son/daughter is missing.	**Il mio bambino ♀/La mia bambina ♂ è scomparso ♂/scomparsa ♀.** eel <u>mee</u>·oh bahm·<u>bee</u>·noh/lah <u>mee</u>·ah bahm·<u>bee</u>·nah eh skohm·<u>pahr</u>·soh ♂/skohm·<u>pahr</u>·sah ♀

I need to *contact my lawyer/make a phone call*.	**Ho bisogno di *chiamare il mio avvocato/ fare una telefonata*.** oh bee·<u>soh</u>·nyoh dee kyah·<u>mah</u>·reh eel <u>mee</u>·oh ahv·voh·<u>kah</u>·toh/ <u>fah</u>·reh <u>oo</u>·nah teh·leh·foh·<u>nah</u>·tah
I'm innocent.	**Sono innocente.** <u>soh</u>·noh een·noh·<u>chehn</u>·teh

You May Hear…

Riempia questo modulo. ree·<u>ehm</u>·pyah <u>kweh</u>·stoh <u>moh</u>·doo·loh	Fill out this form.
Un documento, per favore. oon doh·koo·<u>mehn</u>·toh pehr fah·<u>voh</u>·reh	Your identification, please.
***Quando/Dove* è successo?** <u>kwahn</u>·doh/<u>doh</u>·veh eh soo·<u>cheh</u>·soh	*When/Where* did it happen?
Che aspetto aveva? keh ah·<u>speht</u>·toh ah·<u>veh</u>·vah	What does he/she look like?

> *i* Contact your consulate, ask the concierge at your hotel or ask the tourist information office for telephone numbers of the local ambulance, emergency services and police.

Lost Property and Theft

I'd like to report…	**Vorrei denunciare…** vohr·<u>ray</u> deh·noon·<u>chyah</u>·reh…
– a mugging	**– uno scippo** <u>oo</u>·noh <u>sheep</u>·poh
– a rape	**– uno stupro** <u>oo</u>·noh <u>stoo</u>·proh
– a theft	**– un furto** oon <u>foor</u>·toh
I was *mugged/ robbed.*	**Mi hanno *scippato/derubato.*** mee ahn·noh *sheep·<u>pah</u>·toh/deh·roo·<u>bah</u>·toh*
I lost my…	**Ho perso…** oh <u>pehr</u>·soh…
My…was stolen.	**Mi hanno rubato…** mee <u>ahn</u>·noh roo·<u>bah</u>·toh
– backpack	**– lo zaino** loh <u>dzah</u>·ee·noh
– bicycle	**– la bicicletta** lah bee·chee·<u>kleht</u>·tah
– camera	**– la macchina fotografica** lah <u>mahk</u>·kee·nah foh·toh·<u>grah</u>·fee·kah
– (rental [hire]) car	**– l'auto a noleggio** l·<u>ow</u>·toh ah noh·<u>leh</u>·djoh
– computer	**– il computer** eel kohm·<u>pyoo</u>·tehr
– credit card	**– la carta di credito** lah <u>kahr</u>·tah dee <u>kreh</u>·dee·toh
– jewelry	**– i gioielli** ee joy·<u>ehl</u>·lee
– money	**– il denaro** eel deh·<u>nah</u>·roh
– passport	**– il passaporto** eel pahs·sah·<u>pohr</u>·toh
– purse [handbag]	**– la borsa** lah <u>bohr</u>·sah
– traveler's checks [cheques]	**– i travelers cheques** ee <u>trah</u>·vehl·lehrs chehks
– wallet	**– il portafogli** eel pohr·tah·<u>foh</u>·llyee
I need a police report.	**Ho bisogno di un verbale.** oh bee·<u>soh</u>·nyoh dee oon vehr·<u>bah</u>·leh

Health

I'm sick [ill].	**Sto male.** stoh <u>mah</u>·leh
I need an English-speaking doctor.	**Ho bisogno di un medico che parli inglese.** oh bee·<u>soh</u>·nyoh dee oon <u>meh</u>·dee·koh keh <u>pahr</u>·lee een·<u>gleh</u>·zeh
It hurts here.	**Mi fa male qui.** mee fah <u>mah</u>·leh kwee
I have a stomachache.	**Ho mal di stomaco.** oh mahl dee <u>stoh</u>·mah·koh

Finding a Doctor

Can you recommend a *doctor/dentist*?	**Mi può consigliare un *medico/dentista*?** mee pwoo kohn·see·<u>llyah</u>·reh oon <u>meh</u>·dee·koh/ dehn·<u>tee</u>·stah
Can the doctor come here?	**Il medico può venire?** eel <u>meh</u>·dee·koh pwoh veh·<u>nee</u>·reh
I need an English-speaking doctor.	**Ho bisogno di un medico che parli inglese.** oh bee·<u>soh</u>·nyoh dee oon <u>meh</u>·dee·koh keh <u>pahr</u>·lee een·<u>gleh</u>·zeh
What are the office hours?	**Che orari fate?** keh oh·<u>rah</u>·ree <u>fah</u>·teh
I'd like an appointment for…	**Vorrei un appuntamento…** vohr·<u>ray</u> oon ahp·<u>poon</u>·tah·<u>mehn</u>·toh…
– today	**– per oggi** pehr <u>oh</u>·djee
– tomorrow	**– per domani** pehr doh·<u>mah</u>·nee
– as soon as possible	**– al più presto possibile** ahl pyoo <u>preh</u>·stoh pohs·<u>see</u>·bee·leh
It's urgent.	**È urgente.** eh oor·<u>jehn</u>·teh

Symptoms

I'm bleeding.	**Perdo sangue.** <u>pehr</u>·doh <u>sahn</u>·gweh
I'm constipated.	**Sono costipato.** <u>soh</u>·noh koh·stee·<u>pah</u>·toh
I'm dizzy.	**Mi gira la testa.** mee <u>jee</u>·rah lah <u>teh</u>·stah
I'm nauseous.	**Ho la nausea.** oh lah <u>now</u>·zeh·ah
I'm vomiting.	**Vomito.** <u>voh</u>·mee·toh
It hurts here.	**Mi fa male qui.** mee fah <u>mah</u>·leh kwee
I have…	**Ho…** oh…
– an allergic reaction	**– una reazione allergica** <u>oo</u>·nah reh·ah·<u>tsyoh</u>·neh ahl·<u>lehr</u>·jee·kah
– chest pain	**– un dolore al petto** oon doh·<u>loh</u>·reh ahl <u>peht</u>·toh
– an earache	**– mal d'orecchio** mahl doh·<u>rehk</u>·kyoh
– a fever	**– la febbre** lah <u>fehb</u>·breh
– pain	**– un dolore** oon doh·<u>loh</u>·reh
– a rash	**– un rossore** oon rohs·<u>soh</u>·reh
– a sting	**– una puntura** <u>oo</u>·nah poon·<u>too</u>·rah
– a sprain	**– una storta** <u>oo</u>·nah <u>stohr</u>·tah
– some swelling	**– un gonfiore** oon gohn·<u>fyoh</u>·reh
– a stomach ache	**– mal di stomaco** mahl dee <u>stoh</u>·mah·koh
– sunstroke	**– l'insolazione** leen·soh·lah·<u>tsyoh</u>·neh
I've been sick [ill] for…days.	**Sto male da…giorni.** stoh <u>mah</u>·leh dah…<u>jyohr</u>·nee

▶ For numbers, see page 177.

Health Conditions

I'm...	**Sono...** soh·noh...
– anemic	– **anemico** ♂ /**anemica** ♀ ah·<u>neh</u>·mee·koh ♂ / ah·<u>neh</u>·mee·kah ♀
– asthmatic	– **asmatico** ♂ /**asmatica** ♀ ahz·<u>mah</u>·tee·koh ♂ / ahz·<u>mah</u>·tee·kah ♀
– diabetic	– **diabetico** ♂ /**diabetica** ♀ dee·ah·<u>beh</u>·tee·koh ♂ /dee·ah·<u>beh</u>·tee·kah ♀

I'm allergic to *antibiotics/ penicillin.*

Sono allergico ♂ /**allergica** ♀ *agli antibiotici/alla penicillina.* soh·noh ahl·<u>lehr</u>·jee·koh ♂ /ahl·<u>lehr</u>·jee·kah ♀ *ah·llyee ahn·tee·<u>byoh</u>·tee·chee/<u>ahl</u>·lah peh·nee·cheel·<u>lee</u>·nah*

▶For food items, see page 90.

I have...	**Soffro di...** <u>sohf</u>·froh dee...
– arthritis	– **artrite** ahr·<u>tree</u>·teh
– a heart condition	– **cuore** <u>kwoh</u>·reh
– *high/low* blood pressure	– *alta/bassa* **pressione** <u>ahl</u>·tah/<u>bahs</u>·sah prehs·<u>syoh</u>·neh
I'm on...	**Prendo...** <u>prehn</u>·doh...

Ha allergie? ah ahl·lehr·<u>jee</u>·eh

Are you allergic to anything?

Apra la bocca. <u>ah</u>·prah lah <u>bohk</u>·kah

Open your mouth.

Respiri profondamente. reh·<u>spee</u>·ree proh·fohn·dah·<u>mehn</u>·teh

Breathe deeply.

Vada in ospedale. <u>vah</u>·dah een oh·speh·<u>dah</u>·leh

Go to the hospital.

È... eh...

It's...

– rotto <u>roht</u>·toh

– broken

– contagioso kohn·tah·<u>jyoh</u>·zoh

– contagious

– infetto een·<u>feht</u>·toh

– infected

È una storta. eh oo·nah <u>stohr</u>·tah

It's sprained.

Niente di grave. <u>nyehn</u>·teh dee <u>grah</u>·veh

It's nothing serious.

Hospital

Notify my family, please.	**Avvisi la mia famiglia, per favore.** ahv·<u>vee</u>·zee lah <u>mee</u>·ah fah·<u>mee</u>·llyah pehr fah·<u>voh</u>·reh
I'm in pain.	**Sto male.** stoh <u>mah</u>·leh
I need a doctor/nurse.	**Ho bisogno di *un medico/un'infermiera*.** oh bee·<u>zoh</u>·nyoh dee *oon <u>meh</u>·dee·koh/ oo·neen·fehr·<u>myeh</u>·rah*
When are visiting hours?	**Qual è l'orario delle visite?** kwahl eh loh·<u>rah</u>·ryoh <u>dehl</u>·leh <u>vee</u>·zee·teh
I'm visiting...	**Sto visitando...** stoh vee·zee·<u>tahn</u>·doh...

Dentist

I have a broken tooth.	**Ho un dente rotto.** oh oon <u>dehn</u>·teh <u>roht</u>·toh
I have lost a filling.	**Ho perso un'otturazione.** oh <u>pehr</u>·soh oo·noht·too·rah·<u>tsyoh</u>·neh
I have a toothache.	**Ho mal di denti.** oh mahl dee <u>dehn</u>·tee
Can you fix this denture?	**Può aggiustare la dentiera?** pwoh ah·djoo·<u>stah</u>·reh lah dehn·<u>tyeh</u>·rah

Gynecologist

I have *cramps/a vaginal infection.*	**Ho *i crampi/un'infezione vaginale.*** oh ee <u>krahm</u>·pee/oo·neen·feh·<u>tsyoh</u>·neh vah·jee·<u>nah</u>·leh
I missed my period.	**Non ho avuto il ciclo.** nohn oh ah·<u>voo</u>·toh eel <u>chee</u>·kloh
I'm on the Pill.	**Prendo la pillola.** <u>prehn</u>·doh lah <u>peel</u>·loh·lah
I'm (not) pregnant.	**(Non) Sono incinta.** (nohn) <u>soh</u>·noh een·<u>cheen</u>·tah
My last period was...	**Ho avuto l'ultimo ciclo...** oh ah·<u>voo</u>·toh <u>lool</u>·tee·moh <u>chee</u>·kloh...

Optician

I lost...	**Ho perso...** oh <u>pehr</u>·soh...
– a contact lens	**– una lente a contatto** <u>oo</u>·nah <u>lehn</u>·teh ah kohn·<u>taht</u>·toh
– my glasses	**– gli occhiali** lyee ohk·<u>kyah</u>·lee
– a lens	**– una lente** <u>oo</u>·nah <u>lehn</u>·teh

Payment and Insurance

| How much? | **Quanto costa?** kwahn·toh koh·stah |

Can I pay by
credit card?

Posso pagare con carta di credito?
poh·soh pah·gah·reh kohn kahr·tah dee
kreh·dee·toh

I have insurance. **Ho l'assicurazione.** oh lahs·see·koo·rah·tsyoh·neh

I need a receipt
for my insurance.

Mi serve una ricevuta per l'assicurazione.
mee sehr·veh oo·nah ree·cheh·voo·tah
pehr lahs·see·koo·rah·tsyoh·neh

Pharmacy [Chemist]

Essential

Where's the pharmacy
[chemist]?

Dov'è una farmacia? doh·veh oo·nah
fahr·mah·chee·ah

What time does it
open/close?

A che ora *apre/chiude*? ah keh oh·rah
ah·preh/kyoo·deh

What would you
recommend for...?

Cosa consiglierebbe per...? koh·zah
kohn·see·llyeh·rehb·beh pehr...

How much do I take? **Quanto ne prendo?** kwahn·toh neh
prehn·doh

Can you fill [make up]
this prescription?

Può darmi questo farmaco? pwoh
dahr·mee kweh·stoh fahr·mah·koh

I'm allergic to... **Sono allergico♂/allergica♀ a...** soh·noh
ahl·lehr·jee·koh♂/ahl·lehr·jee·kah♀ ah...

i Pharmacies are usually open from 8:30 a.m.–12:30 p.m. and 3:30 p.m.–7:30 p.m. In larger cities there is often a **farmacia di turno** available; this pharmacy will have extended hours during the week, weekend and on holidays.

In an emergency, dial 118.

Dosage Instructions

How much do I take?	**Quanto ne prendo?** kwahn·toh neh prehn·doh	
How often?	**Con che frequenza?** kohn keh freh·kwehn·tsah	
Is it safe for children?	**È per bambini?** eh pehr bahm·bee·nee	
I'm on…	**Prendo…** prehn·doh…	
Are there side effects?	**Ha effetti collaterali?** ah ehf·feht·tee kohl·lah·teh·rah·lee	

You May See...

UNA/TRE VOLTE AL GIORNO	*once/three* times a day
COMPRESSA	tablet
GOCCIA	drop
CUCCHIAINO	teaspoon
DOPO I/PRIMA DEI/CON I PASTI	*after/before/with* meals
A STOMACO VUOTO	on an empty stomach
DA INGHIOTTIRE INTERA	swallow whole
PUÒ PROVOCARE SONNOLENZA	may cause drowsiness
SOLO PER USO ESTERNO	for external use only

Health Problems

I need something for...

Ho bisogno di qualcosa per... oh bee·<u>soh</u>·nyoh dee kwahl·<u>koh</u>·zah pehr...

– a cold

– **il raffreddore** eel <u>rahf</u>·frehd·<u>doh</u>·reh

– a cough

– **la tosse** lah <u>tohs</u>·seh

– diarrhea

– **la diarrea** lah dee·ahr·<u>reh</u>·ah

– insect bites

– **una puntura d'insetto** <u>oo</u>·nah poon·<u>too</u>·rah deen·<u>seht</u>·toh

– *car/sea/air* motion [travel] sickness

– **il mal *d'auto/di mare/d'aria*** eel mahl *<u>dow</u>·toh/dee <u>mah</u>·reh/<u>dah</u>·ryah*

– a sore throat

– **il mal di gola** eel mahl dee <u>goh</u>·lah

– sunburn

– **una scottatura** <u>oo</u>·nah skoht·tah·<u>too</u>·rah

– an upset stomach

– **lo stomaco in disordine** loh <u>stoh</u>·mah·koh een dee·<u>zohr</u>·dee·neh

Basic Needs

I'd like…   **Vorrei…** vohr·<u>ray</u>…

- acetaminophen   – **del paracetamolo** dehl
  [paracetamol]   pah·rah·cheh·tah·<u>moh</u>·loh

- antiseptic cream   – **una crema antisettica** <u>oo</u>·nah <u>kreh</u>·mah
                              ahn·tee·<u>seht</u>·tee·kah

- aspirin   – **dell'aspirina** dehl·lah·spee·<u>ree</u>·nah

- bandages   – **delle fasce** <u>dehl</u>·leh <u>fah</u>·sheh

- a comb   – **un pettine** oon <u>peht</u>·tee·neh

- condoms   – **dei preservativi** day preh·sehr·vah·<u>tee</u>·vee

- contact lens   – **una soluzione per le lenti a contatto**
  solution   <u>oo</u>·nah soh·loo·<u>tsyoh</u>·neh pehr leh <u>lehn</u>·tee ah
                              kohn·<u>taht</u>·toh

- deodorant   – **un deodorante** oon deh·oh·doh·<u>rahn</u>·teh

- a hairbrush   – **una spazzola** <u>oo</u>·nah <u>spah</u>·tsoh·lah

- hairspray   – **una lacca** <u>oo</u>·nah <u>lahk</u>·kah

- ibuprofen   – **dell'ibuprofene** dehl·lee·boo·proh·<u>feh</u>·neh

- insect repellent   – **un repellente per gli insetti** oon
                              reh·pehl·<u>lehn</u>·teh pehr llyeen·<u>seht</u>·tec

- lotion   – **una lozione** <u>oo</u>·nah loh·<u>tsyoh</u>·neh

- a nail file   – **una limetta per le unghie** <u>oo</u>·nah
                              <u>lee</u>·meht·tah pehr leh <u>oon</u>·ghyeh

- a (disposable) razor   – **una lametta (usa e getta)** <u>oo</u>·nah
                              lah·<u>meht</u>·tah (<u>oo</u>·zah eh <u>jeht</u>·tah)

- razor blades   – **delle lamette per rasoio** <u>dehl</u>·leh
                              lah·<u>meht</u>·teh pehr rah·<u>zoh</u>·yoh

- sanitary napkins   – **un pacco di assorbenti** oon pahk·<u>koh</u>
  [pads]   dee ahs·sohr·<u>behn</u>·tee

– shampoo/ conditioner	– **uno shampoo/un balsamo** <u>oo</u>·noh shahm·<u>pooh</u>/oon <u>bahl</u>·sah·moh
– soap	– **una saponetta** <u>oo</u>·nah sah·poh·<u>neht</u>·tah
– sunscreen	– **un filtro solare** oon <u>feel</u>·troh soh·<u>lah</u>·reh
– tampons	– **una scatola di tamponi** <u>oo</u>·nah <u>ska</u>·toh·lah dee tahm·<u>poh</u>·nee
– tissues	– **dei fazzoletti di carta** day fah·tsoh·<u>leht</u>·tee dee <u>kahr</u>·tah
– toilet paper	– **della carta igienica** <u>dehl</u>·lah <u>kahr</u>·tah ee·<u>jyeh</u>·nee·kah
– toothpaste	– **un dentifricio** oon dehn·tee·<u>free</u>·chyoh

▶ For baby products, see page 154.

Reference

Grammar

In Italian, there are four forms for "you" (taking different verb forms): **tu** (singular) and **voi** (plural) are used informally, when talking to relatives, close friends and children (and among young people); **Lei** (singular) and **loro** (plural) are used in all other cases. If in doubt, use **Lei/loro.** The following abbreviations are used in this section: sing. = singular; pl. = plural; inf. = informal; for. = formal.

Regular Verbs and Their Tenses

There are three verb types: infinitives ending in **-are**, **-ere** and **-ire**, e.g. **parlare** (to speak), **vendere** (to sell) and **dormire** (to sleep). Following are sample conjugations for each verb type.

PARLARE (to speak, to talk)		Present	Past	Future
I	**io**	parl**o**	ho parlato	parl**erò**
you (sing.) (inf.)	**tu**	parl**i**	hai parlato	parl**erai**
he/she/you (sing.) (for.)	**lui/lei/Lei**	parl**a**	ha parlato	parl**erà**
we	**noi**	parl**iamo**	abbiamo parlato	parl**eremo**
you (pl.) (inf.)	**voi**	parl**ate**	avete parlato	parl**erete**
they/you (pl.) (for.)	**loro**	parl**ano**	hanno parlato	parl**eranno**

VENDERE (to sell)		Present	Past	Future
I	**io**	vend**o**	ho venduto	vend**erò**
you (sing.) (inf.)	**tu**	vend**i**	hai venduto	vend**erai**
he/she/you (sing.) (for.)	**lui/lei/Lei**	vend**e**	ha venduto	vend**erà**
we	**noi**	vend**iamo**	abbiamo venduto	vend**eremo**
you (pl.) (inf.)	**voi**	vend**ete**	avete venduto	vend**erete**
they/you (pl.) (for.)	**loro**	vend**ono**	hanno venduto	vend**eranno**

DORMIRE (to sleep)		Present	Past	Future
I	**io**	dorm**o**	ho dormito	dormir**ò**
you (sing.) (inf.)	**tu**	dorm**i**	hai dormito	dormir**ai**
he/she/you (sing.) (for.)	**lui/lei/Lei**	dorm**e**	ha dormito	dormir**à**
we	**noi**	dorm**iamo**	abbiamo dormito	dormir**emo**
you (pl.) (inf.)	**voi**	dorm**ite**	avete dormito	dormir**ete**
they/you (pl.) (for.)	**loro**	dorm**ono**	hanno dormito	dormir**anno**

Irregular Verbs

There are many irregular verbs whose forms do not follow the regular patterns. Following are the present, past and future forms of **essere** (to be) and **avere** (to have).

ESSERE (to be)		Present	Past	Future
I	**io**	sono	sono stato	sarò
you (sing.) (inf.)	**tu**	sei	sei stato	sarai
he/she/you (sing.) (for)	**lui/lei/Lei**	è	è stato	sarà
we	**noi**	siamo	siamo stati	saremo
you (pl.) (inf.)	**voi**	siete	siete stati	sarete
they/you (pl.) (for.)	**loro**	sono	sono stati	saranno

AVERE (to have)		Present	Past	Future
I	**io**	ho	ho avuto	avrò
you (sing.) (inf.)	**tu**	hai	hai avuto	avrai
he/she/you (sing.) (for)	**lui/lei/Lei**	ha	ha avuto	avrà
we	**noi**	abbiamo	abbiamo avuto	avremo
you (pl.) (inf.)	**voi**	avete	avete avuto	avrete
they/you (pl.) (for.)	**loro**	hanno	hanno avuto	avranno

Nouns and Articles

Generally nouns ending in **–o** are masculine, their plural ending changing to **–i**. Those ending in **–a** are usually feminine, their plural ending changing to **–e**. Nouns ending in **–e** can be either gender changing to **–i** in the plural.

The definite articles (the) are **il** ♂ and **la** ♀; **l'** is used for singular masculine or feminine nouns that begin with a vowel. The plural forms are **i** ♂ and **le** ♀. When a masculine noun begins with **z** or **s** + consonant, the singular article changes to **lo**, the plural to **gli**. **Gli** is also used before plural masculine nouns that begin with a vowel.

The indefinite articles (a, an) also indicate gender: a masculine noun uses **un**, or **uno** when the noun begins with **z** or **s** + consonant. The feminine noun takes **una**, or **un'** when the noun begins with a vowel.

When prepositions are followed by definite articles, they sometimes combine to form one word. For example: **di** + **el** = **del**; **di** + **lo** = **dello**; **di** + **l'** = **dell'**; **di** + **i** = **dei**; **di** + **gli** = **degli**; **di** + **la** = **della**; **di** + **le** = **delle**.

Word Order

Italian sentences generally follow the subject-verb-object pattern, as in English.

Example: **Vorrei un taxi subito.** I'd like a taxi now.

In Italian, adjectives usually follow the noun.

Example: **un'auto economica** a cheap car (literally, a car cheap)

To form a question in Italian, you can raise the intonation at the end of the sentence, as in English, or use a question word.

Examples:

Lei parla italiano./Lei parla italiano?

You speak Italian./Do you speak Italian?

Quanto costa?

How much?

Negations

To form the negative, use **non** before the conjugated verb.

Example: **Parlo inglese./Non parlo inglese.**

I speak English./I don't speak English.

Imperatives

The imperative, or command form, of Italian verbs is used to give orders or advice. Signs are often in the imperative form. It is formed by adding a specific ending to the "stem" of the verb (add **–i** to **–are** verbs, and **–a** to **–ere** and **–ire** verbs). To say the negative, add **non** before the verb. The following are the polite ways to say common commands in Italian:

Fermi!	**Avanti!**	**Non parli!**
Stop!	Go!	Don't speak!

To say "Let's…", add **–iamo** to the stem of the verb.

Andiamo!	**Finiamo!**
Let's go!	Let's finish!

Possessive Pronouns and Adjectives

The following are the Italian forms of possessive pronouns/ adjectives. Note that the gender and number agree with the noun, not the speaker.

	masculine, singular	masculine, plural	feminine, singular	feminine, plural
my, mine	**il mio**	**i miei**	**la mia**	**le mie**
your, yours	**il tuo**	**i tuoi**	**la tua**	**le tue**
his, her, hers, its, yours (sing.) (for.)	**il suo**	**i suoi**	**la sua**	**le sue**
our, ours	**il nostro**	**i nostri**	**la nostra**	**le nostre**
your, yours	**il vostro**	**i vostri**	**la vostra**	**le vostre**
their, theirs, yours (pl.) (for.)	**il loro**	**i loro**	**la loro**	**le loro**

Adjectives

Adjectives modify nouns and must agree with the noun in both gender and number. Adjectives ending in **–o** can have four forms, matching the noun:

Masculine, singular: end in **–o: ragazzo italiano** (Italian boy)

Masculine, plural: end in **–i: ragazzi italiani** (Italian boys)

Feminine, singular: end in **–a: signora italiana** (Italian woman)

Feminine, plural: end in **–e: signore italiane** (Italian women)

Adjectives ending in **–e** are the same for masculine and feminine singular, and change to **–i** in the masculine and feminine plural forms.

Example: **ragazzo inglese** (English boy); **ragazza inglese** (English girl); **ragazzi inglesi** (English boys); **ragazze inglesi** (English girls)

Comparative and Superlative

To say "more", use **più**. To say "less", use **meno**. To say "the most" or "the least", use **più** or **meno**, respectively, preceded by the definite article.

Examples:

casa grande/casa più grande/la casa più grande

large house/larger house/the largest house

borsa piccola/borsa più piccola/la borsa più piccola

small bag/smaller bag/the smallest bag

Adverbs and Adverbial Expressions

Some Italian adverbs are formed by adding **–mente** to the feminine singular form of the adjective.

Example: **lento**♂ **/lenta**♀ (slow), **lentamente** (slowly)

If the adjective ends in **–le** or **–re**, drop the **–e** and add **–mente**.

Example: **facile** (easy), **facilmente** (easily)

Numbers

Essential

0	**zero** <u>dzeh</u>·roh
1	**uno** <u>oo</u>·noh
2	**due** <u>doo</u>·eh
3	**tre** treh
4	**quattro** <u>kwaht</u>·troh
5	**cinque** <u>cheen</u>·kweh
6	**sei** say
7	**sette** <u>seht</u>·teh
8	**otto** <u>oht</u>·toh
9	**nove** <u>noh</u>·veh
10	**dieci** <u>dyeh</u>·chee
11	**undici** <u>oon</u>·dee·chee
12	**dodici** <u>doh</u>·dee·chee
13	**tredici** <u>treh</u>·dee·chee
14	**quattordici** kwaht·<u>tohr</u>·dee·chee
15	**quindici** <u>kween</u>·dee·chee
16	**sedici** <u>seh</u>·dee·chee
17	**diciassette** dee·chyahs·<u>seht</u>·teh
18	**diciotto** dee·<u>chyoht</u>·toh
19	**diciannove** dee·chyahn·<u>noh</u>·veh
20	**venti** <u>vehn</u>·tee
21	**ventuno** vehn·<u>too</u>·noh
22	**ventidue** vehn·tee·<u>doo</u>·eh
30	**trenta** <u>trehn</u>·tah

31	**trentuno** trehn·<u>too</u>·noh
40	**quaranta** kwah·<u>rahn</u>·tah
50	**cinquanta** cheen·<u>kwahn</u>·tah
60	**sessanta** sehs·<u>sahn</u>·tah
70	**settanta** seht·<u>tahn</u>·tah
80	**ottanta** oht·<u>tahn</u>·tah
90	**novanta** noh·<u>vahn</u>·tah
100	**cento** <u>chehn</u>·toh
101	**centuno** chehn·<u>too</u>·noh
200	**duecento** doo·eh·<u>chehn</u>·toh
500	**cinquecento** cheen·kweh·<u>chehn</u>·toh
1,000	**mille** <u>meel</u>·leh
10,000	**diecimila** dyeh·chee·<u>mee</u>·lah
1,000,000	**milione** mee·<u>lyoh</u>·neh

Ordinal Numbers

first	**primo** <u>pree</u>·moh
second	**secondo** seh·<u>kohn</u>·doh
third	**terzo** <u>tehr</u>·tsoh
fourth	**quarto** <u>kwahr</u>·toh
fifth	**quinto** <u>kween</u>·toh
once	**una volta** <u>oo</u>·nah <u>vohl</u>·tah
twice	**due volte** <u>doo</u>·eh <u>vohl</u>·teh
three times	**tre volte** treh <u>vohl</u>·teh

Time

What time is it?	**Che ore sono?** keh <u>oh</u>·reh <u>soh</u>·noh
It's noon [midday].	**È mezzogiorno.** eh meh·dzoh·<u>jyohr</u>·noh
At midnight.	**A mezzanotte.** ah meh·dzah·<u>noht</u>·teh
From one o'clock to two o'clock.	**Dall'una alle due.** dahl·<u>loo</u>·nah <u>ahl</u>·leh <u>doo</u>·eh
Five after [past] three.	**Le tre e cinque.** leh treh eh <u>cheen</u>·kweh
A quarter to three.	**Sono le tre meno un quarto.** <u>soh</u>·noh leh treh <u>meh</u>·noh oon <u>kwahr</u>·toh
5:30 a.m./5:30 p.m.	**le cinque e mezzo/le diciassette e trenta** leh <u>cheen</u>·kweh eh <u>meh</u>·dzoh/leh <u>dee</u>·chyahs·<u>seht</u>·teh eh <u>trehn</u>·tah

Days

Monday	**lunedì** loon·eh·<u>dee</u>
Tuesday	**martedì** mahr·teh·<u>dee</u>
Wednesday	**mercoledì** mehr·koh·leh·<u>dee</u>
Thursday	**giovedì** jyoh·veh·<u>dee</u>
Friday	**venerdì** veh·nehr·<u>dee</u>
Saturday	**sabato** <u>sah</u>·bah·toh
Sunday	**domenica** doh·<u>meh</u>·nee·kah

Lunedì (Monday) is the first day of the week; **domenica** (Sunday) is the last. Italian does not capitalize the names of days.

Dates

yesterday	**ieri** <u>yeh</u>·ree
today	**oggi** <u>oh</u>·djee
tomorrow	**domani** doh·<u>mah</u>·nee
day	**giorno** <u>jyohr</u>·noh
week	**settimana** seht·tee·<u>mah</u>·nah
month	**mese** <u>meh</u>·zeh
year	**anno** <u>ahn</u>·noh

Months

January	**gennaio** jehn·<u>nah</u>·yoh
February	**febbraio** fehb·<u>brah</u>·yoh
March	**marzo** <u>mahr</u>·tsoh
April	**aprile** ah·<u>pree</u>·leh

May	**maggio** <u>mah</u>·djoh
June	**giugno** <u>jyoo</u>·nyoh
July	**luglio** <u>loo</u>·llyoh
August	**agosto** ah·<u>goh</u>·stoh
September	**settembre** seht·<u>tehm</u>·breh
October	**ottobre** oht·<u>toh</u>·breh
November	**novembre** noh·<u>vehm</u>·breh
December	**dicembre** dee·<u>chem</u>·breh

Seasons

in/during...	**in/durante...** een/doo·<u>rahn</u>·teh...
– the spring	– **la primavera** lah pree·mah·<u>veh</u>·rah
– the summer	– **l'estate** leh·<u>stah</u>·teh
– the fall [autumn]	– **l'autunno** l·ow·<u>toon</u>·noh
– the winter	– **l'inverno** leen·<u>vehr</u>·noh

Holidays

January 1: **Capodanno** New Year's Day
January 6: **Epifania** Epiphany
April 25: **Festa della Liberazione** Liberation Day
May 1: **Festa dei Lavoratori** Labor Day
August 15: **Ferragosto** Assumption Day
November 1: **Ognissanti** All Saints Day
December 8: **Immacolata Concezione** Immaculate Conception
December 25: **Natale** Christmas Day
December 26: **Santo Stefano** St. Stephen's Day
Moveable dates include:
Venerdì Santo Good Friday
Pasqua Easter Day
Pasquetta Easter Monday

Conversion Tables

When you know	Multiply by	To find
ounces	28.3	grams
pounds	0.45	kilograms
inches	2.54	centimeters
feet	0.3	meters
miles	1.61	kilometers
square inches	6.45	sq. centimeters
square feet	0.09	sq. meters
square miles	2.59	sq. kilometers
pints (U.S./Brit)	0.47/0.56	liters
gallons (U.S./Brit)	3.8/4.5	liters
Fahrenheit	5/9, after −32	Centigrade
Centigrade	9/5, then +32	Fahrenheit

Mileage

1 km	− 0.62 mi	20 km	− 12.4 mi
5 km	− 3.10 mi	50 km	− 31.0 mi
10 km	− 6.20 mi	100 km	− 61.0 mi

Measurement

1 gram (gr)	**1 grammo**	= 0.035 oz.
1/10 of a kilo	**etto** (sing.)/**etti** (pl.)	= 0.22 lb
1 kilogram (kg)	**1 chilo**	= 2.2 lb
1 liter (l)	**1 litro**	= 1.06 U.S./ 0.88 Brit. quarts
1 centimeter (cm)	**1 centimetro**	= 0.4 inch
1 meter (m)	**1 metro**	= 3.28 ft.
1 kilometer (km)	**1 chilometró**	= 0.62 mile

Temperature

-40° C – -40° F	-1° C – 30° F	20° C – 68° F
-30° C – -22° F	0° C – 32° F	25° C – 77° F
-20° C – -4° F	5° C – 41° F	30° C – 86° F
-10° C – 14° F	10° C – 50° F	35° C – 95° F
-5° C – 23° F	15° C – 59° F	

Oven Temperature

100° C – 212° F	177° C – 350° F
121° C – 250° F	204° C – 400° F
149° C – 300° F	260° C – 500° F

Related Websites

www.tsa.gov
U.S. Transportation Security Administration

www.caa.co.uk
U.K. Civil Aviation Authority

www.trenitalia.it
Italian train schedules

www.raileurope.com
Rail Europe website

www.italyferry.com
Italian ferry information

www.agriturismoinitalia.com
agritourism information

www.b-brm.it
bed and breakfast information

www.hihostels.com
Hostelling International website

www.posteitaliane.com
official post office website for Italy

English–Italian Dictionary

A

a.m. del mattino
abbey l'abbazia
accept v accettare
access l'accesso
accident l'incidente
accommodation l'alloggio
account il conto
acupuncture l'agopuntura
adapter l'adattatore
address l'indirizzo
admission l'ingresso
after dopo; ~noon il pomeriggio; ~shave il dopobarba
age l'età
agency l'agenzia
AIDS l'AIDS
air l'aria; ~ conditioning l'aria condizionata; ~ pump la pompa dell'aria; ~line la compagnia aerea; ~mail la posta aerea; ~plane l'aereo; ~port l'aeroporto
aisle il corridoio; ~ seat il posto sul corridoio
allergic allergico; ~ reaction la reazione allergica
allow v permettere
alone solo
alter v modificare
alternate route il percorso alternativo
aluminum foil la carta stagnola
amazing straordinario
ambulance l'ambulanza

American americano
amusement park il lunapark
anemic anemico
anesthesia l'anestesia
animal l'animale
ankle la caviglia
antibiotic l'antibiotico
antiques store il negozio d'antiquariato
antiseptic cream la crema antisettica
anything qualsiasi cosa
apartment l'appartamento
appendix (body part) l'appendice
appetizer l'antipasto
appointment l'appuntamento
arcade la sala giochi
area code il prefisso
arm il braccio
aromatherapy l'aromaterapia
around (the corner) dietro di
arrivals (airport) gli arrivi
arrive v arrivare
artery l'arteria
arthritis l'artrite
art l'arte
aspirin l'aspirina
asthmatic asmatico
ATM il bancomat
attack l'aggressione
attend v frequentare
attraction (place) l'attrattiva
attractive attraente
Australia Australia
Australian australiano
automatic automatico; ~ car l'auto col cambio automatico
available libero

B

baby il bebè; **~ bottle** il biberon;
  ~ wipe la salvietta per neonati;
  ~sitter la babysitter
back (body part) la schiena; **~ache**
  il mal di schiena; **~pack** lo zaino
bag la borsa
baggage il bagaglio; **~ claim** il
  ritiro bagagli; **~ ticket** lo
  scontrino bagagli
bakery la panetteria
ballet lo spettacolo di danza
bandage la benda
bank la banca
bar il bar
barbecue il barbecue
barber il barbiere
baseball il baseball
basket (grocery store) il cestino
basketball il basketball
bathroom il bagno
battery la batteria
battleground il campo di battaglia
be *v* essere
beach la spiaggia
beautiful bello
bed il letto; **~ and breakfast** la
  pensione
begin *v* iniziare
before prima
beginner il principiante
behind dietro
beige beige
belt la cintura
berth la cuccetta
best il migliore
better migliore
bicycle la bicicletta
big grande

bigger più grande
bike route il percorso ciclabile
bikini il bikini; **~ wax** la ceretta
  all'inguine
bill *v* (charge) fatturare;
  ~ *n* (money) la banconota; **~** *n*
  (of sale) il conto
bird l'uccello
birthday il compleanno
black nero
bladder la vescica
bland insipido
blanket la coperta
bleed *v* sanguinare
blood il sangue; **~ pressure** la
  pressione sanguigna
blouse la camicetta
blue blu
board *v* imbarcarsi
boarding pass la carta d'imbarco
boat la barca
bone l'osso
book il libro; **~store** la libreria
boots gli stivali
boring noioso
botanical garden il giardino
  botanico
bother *v* infastidire
bottle la bottiglia;
  ~ opener l'apribottiglie
bowl la coppa
box la scatola
boxing match l'incontro di boxe
boy il ragazzo; **~friend** il ragazzo
bra il reggiseno
bracelet il braccialetto
brakes (car) i freni
break *v* rompere; **~-in**
  (burglary) il furto con scasso;
  ~down il guasto

breakfast la colazione
breast il petto; ~**feed** v allattare
breathe v respirare
bridge il ponte
briefs (clothing) lo slip
bring v portare
British inglese
broken rotto
brooch la spilla
broom la scopa
brother il fratello
brown marrone
bug l'insetto
building l'edificio
burn v bruciare
bus l'autobus; ~ **station** la
   stazione degli autobus;
   ~ **stop** la fermata del bus;
   ~ **ticket** il biglietto del bus;
   ~ **tour** l'escursione in
   pullman
business il lavoro; ~ **card** il
   biglietto da visita; ~ **center** il
   centro business; ~ **class** la
   classe business; ~ **hours** l'orario
   d'apertura
butcher il macellaio
buttocks le natiche
buy v comprare
bye ciao

C

cabaret il cabaret
cabin la cabina
cable car la funivia
cafe il caffè
call v chiamare; ~ n la chiamata
calories le calorie

camera la macchina fotografica;
   digital ~ la macchina fotografica
   digitale; ~ **case** l'astuccio della
   macchina fotografica; ~ **store** il
   negozio di fotografia
camp v campeggiare; ~ **stove** il
   fornello da campeggio; ~**site** il
   campeggio
can opener l'apriscatole
Canada il Canada
Canadian canadese
cancel v annullare
candy le caramelle
canned good lo scatolame
canyon il canalone
car l'auto; ~ **hire** [BE]
   l'autonoleggio; ~ **park**
   [BE] il parcheggio; ~ **rental**
   l'autonoleggio; ~ **seat** il
   seggiolino per auto
carafe la caraffa
card la carta; **ATM** ~ il bancomat;
   credit ~ la carta di credito; **debit**
   ~ il bancomat; **phone** ~ la
   scheda telefonica
carry on board v [BE] portare
   a bordo
carry-on il bagaglio a mano
cart (grocery store) il carrello;
   ~ **(luggage)** il carrello
carton il cartone; ~ **of**
   cigarettes la stecca di sigarette
case (container) la cassa
cash v incassare; ~ n i contanti;
   ~ **advance** l'acconto
cashier il cassiere
casino il casinò
castle il castello
cathedral la cattedrale
cave la grotta

CD il CD
cell phone il telefonino
Celsius Celsius
centimeter il centimetro
certificate il certificato
chair la sedia; ~ lift la seggiovia
change v (buses) cambiare;
~ v (money) cambiare;
~ v (baby) cambiare;
~ n (money) il cambio
charcoal il carbone
charge v (credit card)
addebitare; ~ n (cost) il
costo
cheap economico; ~er più
economico
check v (on something)
controllare; ~ v (luggage)
controllare; ~ n (payment)
l'assegno; ~-in (hotel/airport)
il check-in; ~ing account il
conto corrente; ~-out (hotel) il
pagamento del conto
Cheers! Salute!
chemical toilet il WC da
campeggio
chemist [BE] la farmacia
cheque [BE] l'assegno
chest (body part) il petto;
~ pain il dolore al petto
chewing gum la gomma da
masticare
child il bambino; ~ seat il
seggiolone; ~'s menu il menù
per bambino; ~'s portion la
porzione per bambino
Chinese cinese
chopsticks i bastoncini cinesi
church la chiesa
cigar il sigaro
cigarette la sigaretta

class la classe; business ~
la classe business; economy
~ la classe economica; first
~ la prima classe
classical music la musica
classica
clean v pulire; ~ adj pulito; ~ing
product il prodotto per la pulizia;
~ing supplies i prodotti per la
pulizia
clear v (on an ATM) cancellare
cliff la scogliera
cling film [BE] la pellicola per
alimenti
close v (a shop) chiudere
close vicino
closed chiuso
clothing l'abbigliamento;
~ store il negozio
d'abbigliamento
club il club
coat il cappotto
coffee shop il caffè
coin la moneta
colander la scolapasta
cold (sickness) il raffreddore;
~ (temperature) freddo
colleague il collega
cologne la colonia
color il colore
comb il pettine
come v venire
complaint il reclamo
computer il computer
concert il concerto; ~ hall la sala
da concerti
condition (medical) la condizione
conditioner il balsamo
condom il preservativo
conference la conferenza

confirm *v* confermare
congestion la congestione
connect *v* (internet) collegarsi
connection (internet)
il collegamento; ~ (flight)
la coincidenza
constipated costipato
consulate il consolato
consultant il consulente
contact *v* contattare; ~ lens la
lente a contatto; ~ lens solution la
soluzione per lenti a contatto
contagious contagioso
convention hall la sala congressi
conveyor belt il nastro
trasportatore
cook *v* cucinare
cooking gas il gas per cucina
cool (temperature) fresco
copper il rame
corkscrew il cavatappi
cost *v* costare
cot il lettino
cotton il cotone
cough *v* tossire; ~ *n* la tosse
country code il prefisso del paese
cover charge il coperto
crash *v* (car) fare un incidente
cream (ointment) la crema
credit card la carta di credito
crew neck a girocollo
crib la culla
crystal il cristallo
cup la tazza
currency la valuta; ~ exchange
il cambio valuta; ~ exchange
office l'ufficio di cambio
current account [BE] il conto
corrente
customs la dogana

cut *v* (hair) tagliare;
~ *n* (injury) il taglio
cute carino
cycling il ciclismo

D

damage *v* danneggiare;
~d danneggiato
dance *v* ballare; ~ club il club di
ballo; ~ing il ballo
dangerous pericoloso
dark scuro
date (calendar) la data
day il giorno
deaf sordo
debit card il bancomat
deck chair la sedia a sdraio
declare *v* dichiarare
decline *v* (credit card) rifiutare
deeply profondamente
degrees (temperature) i gradi
delay *v* ritardare
delete *v* (computer) eliminare
delicatessen la gastronomia
delicious squisito
denim i jeans
dentist il dentista
denture la dentiera
deodorant il deodorante
department store il grande
magazzino
departures (airport) le partenze
deposit *v* depositare;
~ (bank) *n* il deposito;
~ (to reserve a room) il deposito
desert il deserto
detergent il detersivo
develop *v* (film) sviluppare

diabetic diabetico
dial *v* comporre il numero
diamond il diamante
diaper il pannolino
diarrhea la diarrea
diesel il diesel
difficult difficile
digital digitale; **~ camera** la macchina fotografica digitale; **~ photos** le foto digitali; **~ prints** le stampe digitali
dining room la sala da pranzo
dinner la cena
direction la direzione
dirty sporco
disabled il disabile; **~ accessible [BE]** accessibile ai disabili
disconnect *v* **(computer)** scollegare
discount lo sconto
dish (kitchen) il piatto; **~washer** la lavastoviglie; **~washing liquid** il detersivo per i piatti
display lo schermo; **~ case** la vetrinetta
disposable usa e getta; **~ razor** la lametta usa e getta
dive *v* tuffarsi; **~ing equipment** l'attrezzatura subacquea
divorce *v* divorziare
dizzy stordito
doctor il medico
doll la bambola
dollar (U.S.) il dollaro
domestic domestico; **~ flight** il volo nazionale
door la porta

dormitory il dormitorio
double bed il letto matrimoniale
downtown (direction) il centro; **~ area** il centro
dozen la dozzina
drag lift lo ski lift
dress (piece of clothing) il vestito; **~ code** il codice di abbigliamento
drink *v* bere; **~** *n* la bevanda; **~ menu** il menù delle bevande; **~ing water** l'acqua potabile
drive *v* guidare
driver's license number il numero di patente
drop (medicine) la goccia
drowsiness la sonnolenza
dry cleaner il lavasecco
dubbed doppiato
during durante
duty (tax) la tassa; **~ free** duty free
DVD il DVD

E

ear l'orecchio; **~ache** il mal d'orecchio
earlier prima
early presto
earrings gli orecchini
east est
easy facile
eat *v* mangiare
economy class la classe economica
elbow il gomito
electric outlet la presa elettrica
elevator l'ascensore

e-mail v inviare e-mail; ~ n
l'e-mail; ~ **address** l'indirizzo
e-mail
emergency l'emergenza;
~ **exit** l'uscita d'emergenza
empty v svuotare
enamel (jewelry) lo smalto
end v finire
English inglese
engrave v incidere
enjoy v godersi
enter v entrare
entertainment l'intrattenimento
entrance l'entrata
envelope la busta
equipment l'attrezzatura
escalators le scale mobili
estate car [BE] la station
wagon
e-ticket il biglietto elettronico
EU resident il residente UE
euro l'euro
evening la sera
excess l'eccesso
exchange v **(money)** cambiare;
~ n **(place)** il cambio;
~ **rate** il tasso di cambio
excursion l'escursione
excuse v scusare
exhausted esausto
exit v uscire; ~ n l'uscita
expensive caro
expert esperto
exposure (film) la posa
express espresso; ~ **bus** il
bus espresso; ~ **train** il treno
espresso
extension (phone) l'interno
extra extra; ~ **large** extra large
extract v **(tooth)** estrarre

eye l'occhio
eyebrow wax la ceretta per
sopracciglie

F

face il viso
facial la pulizia del viso
family la famiglia
fan (appliance) il ventilatore;
~ **(souvenir)** il ventaglio
far lontano; ~-**sighted**
ipermetrope
farm la fattoria
fast veloce; ~ **food** il fast
food
faster più veloce
fat free senza grassi
father il padre
fax v inviare per fax; ~ n il fax;
~ **number** il numero di fax
fee la tariffa
feed v dare da mangiare
ferry il traghetto
fever la febbre
field (sports) il campo
fill v riempire; ~ **out** v
(form) compilare; ~**ing**
(tooth) l'otturazione
film (camera) il rullino
fine (fee for breaking law)
la multa
finger il dito; ~**nail** l'unghia
fire il fuoco; ~ **department**
i vigili del fuoco; ~ **door** la porta
antincendio
first primo; ~ **class** la prima
classe
fit (clothing) v andare bene
fitting room il camerino

fix *v* (repair) riparare
flashlight la torcia elettrica
flat tire la gomma a terra
flight il volo
floor il pavimento
flower il fiore
folk music la musica folk
food il cibo
foot il piede
football game [BE] la partita di football
for per
forecast la previsione
forest il bosco
fork la forchetta
form il modulo
formula (baby) il latte in polvere
fort la fortezza
fountain la fontana
free libero
freezer il freezer
fresh fresco
friend l'amico
frying pan la padella
full-service il servizio completo
full-time a tempo pieno

G

game la partita
garage il garage
garbage bag il sacchetto per la spazzatura
gas (cooking) il gas per cucina; ~ **(heating)** il gas; ~ **station** la stazione del servizio; ~ **(vehicle)** la benzina

gate (airport) l'uscita
gay gay; ~ **bar** il bar per gay; ~ **club** il club per gay
gel (hair) il gel
get off *v* **(a train/bus/subway)** scendere
get to *v* arrivare
gift il regalo; ~ **shop** il negozio di articoli da regalo
girl la ragazza; ~**friend** la ragazza
give *v* dare
glass (drinking) il bicchiere; ~ **(material)** il vetro; ~**es** gli occhiali
go *v* **(somewhere)** andare
gold l'oro
golf golf; ~ **course** il campo da golf; ~ **club** la mazza; ~ **tournament** la gara di golf
good *n* il bene; ~ *adj* buono; ~ **afternoon** buon pomeriggio; ~ **evening** buonasera; ~ **morning** buongiorno; ~**bye** arrivederla; ~**s** le merci
gram il grammo
grandchild il nipote
grandparent il nonno
gray grigio
green verde
grocery store il fruttivendolo
ground floor il pianterreno
groundcloth [groundsheet BE] il telone impermeabile
group il gruppo
guide la guida; ~ **book** la guida; ~ **dog** il cane da guida
gym la palestra
gynecologist il ginecologo

H

hair i capelli; ~ dryer
l'asciugacapelli; ~ salon il
parrucchiere; ~brush la spazzola
; ~ cut il taglio; ~spray la lacca;
~style l'acconciatura; ~stylist il
parrucchiere
half la metà; ~ hour la mezz'ora;
~-kilo il mezzo chilo
hammer il martello
hand la mano; ~ luggage il
bagaglio a mano; ~bag la
borsetta
handicapped il disabile;
~-accessible accessibile ai
disabili
hangover la sbornia
happy felice
hat il cappello
have v avere
head (body part) la testa;
~ache il mal di testa;
~phones gli auricolari
health la salute; ~ food
store l'erboristeria
heart il cuore; ~ condition il
disturbo cardiaco
heat il calore; ~er il radiatore
hello salve
helmet il casco
help v aiutare; ~ n l'aiuto
here qui
heterosexual eterosessuale
hi ciao
high alto; ~chair il seggiolone;
~-heeled shoes le scarpe col
tacco alto; ~way l'autostrada
hiking boots gli scarponi da
montagna
hill la collina

hire v [BE] noleggiare;
~ car [BE] l'auto a noleggio
hitchhike v fare l'autostop
hockey l'hockey
holiday [BE] la vacanza
horse track l'ippodromo
hospital l'ospedale
hostel l'ostello
hot (temperature) caldo;
~ (spicy) piccante;
~ springs le terme;
~ water l'acqua calda
hotel l'hotel
hour l'ora
house la casa; ~hold goods
gli articoli casalinghi; ~keeping
services i servizi di pulizia
domestica
how come; ~ much quanto
hug v abbracciare
hungry affamato
hurt il dolore
husband il marito

I

ibuprofen l'ibuprofene
ice il ghiaccio; ~ hockey
l'hockey su ghiaccio
icy gelato
identification l'identificazione
ill malato
in in
include v includere
indoor pool la piscina
interna
inexpensive a buon mercato
infected infetto
information (phone) le informazioni;
~ desk l'ufficio informazioni

insect insetto; ~ **bite** la puntura
d'insetto; ~ **repellent** il
repellente per gli insetti
insert *v* inserire
insomnia l'insonnia
instant message il messaggio
istantaneo
insulin l'insulina
insurance l'assicurazione; ~ **card**
la tessera dell'assicurazione;
~ **company** la compagnia di
assicurazione
interesting interessante
intermediate intermedio
international (airport area)
internazionale; ~ **flight** il volo
internazionale; ~ **student card** la
tessera internazionale dello studente
internet l'Internet; ~ **cafe**
l'Internet caffè; ~ **service** il
servizio Internet; **wireless** ~ il
collegamento wireless a Internet
interpreter l'interprete
intersection l'incrocio
intestine l'intestino
introduce *v* presentare
invoice [BE] la fattura
Ireland l'Irlanda
Irish irlandese
iron *v* stirare; ~ *n* (clothes) il
ferro da stiro
Italian italiano
Italy l'Italia

J

jacket la giacca
jar il vaso
jaw la mascella
jazz il jazz; ~ **club** il club jazz

jeans i jeans
jet ski l'acquascooter
jeweler il gioielliere
jewelry la gioielleria
join *v* unire
joint (body part) la giuntura

K

key la chiave; ~ **card** la chiave
elettronica; ~ **ring** il portachiavi
kiddie pool la piscina per bambini
kidney (body part) il rene
kilo il chilo; ~**gram** il chilogrammo;
~**meter** il chilometro
kiss *v* baciare
kitchen la cucina; ~ **foil** la carta
stagnola
knee il ginocchio
knife il coltello

L

lace il pizzo
lactose intolerant intollerante al
lattosio
lake il lago
large grande
larger più grande
last ultimo
late (time) tardi
later più tardi
launderette [BE] la lavanderia a
gettone
laundromat la lavanderia a
gettone
laundry la lavanderia;
~ **facility** il locale lavanderia;
~ **service** il servizio di lavanderia

lawyer l'avvocato
leather la pelle
leave v partire
left (direction) a sinistra
leg la gamba
lens la lente
less meno
lesson la lezione
letter la lettera
library la biblioteca
life la vita; ~ jacket il giubbotto di salvataggio; ~guard il bagnino
lift (ride) il passaggio; ~ [BE] l'ascensore; ~ pass il lift pass
light (overhead) la lampada; ~ v (cigarette) accendere; ~bulb la lampadina; ~er l'accendino
like v (someone) piacere
line (train) la linea
linen il lino
lip il labbro
liquor store l'enoteca
liter il litro
little piccolo
live v vivere
liver (body part) il fegato
loafers i mocassini
local locale
lock v chiudere; ~ n la serratura
locker l'armadietto
log off v (computer) fare il logoff
log on v (computer) fare il logon
long lungo; ~ sleeves le maniche lunghe; ~-sighted [BE] ipermetrope
look v guardare
lose v (something) perdere
lost perso; ~ and found l'ufficio oggetti smarriti

lotion la lozione
louder più forte
love v (someone) amare; ~ n l'amore
low basso; ~er più basso
luggage il bagaglio; ~ cart il carrello bagagli; ~ locker l'armadietto dei bagagli; ~ ticket lo scontrino dei bagagli; hand ~ [BE] il bagaglio a mano
lunch il pranzo
lung il polmone

M

magazine la rivista
magnificent magnifico
mail v spedire; ~ n la posta; ~box la cassetta della posta
main principale; ~ attraction l'attrattiva principale; ~ course il piatto principale
make up [BE] (a prescription) il trucco
mall il centro commerciale
man l'uomo
manager il responsabile
manicure il manicure
manual car l'auto col cambio manuale
map la cartina
market il mercato
married sposato
marry v sposare
mass (church service) la messa
massage il massaggio
match n (wooden stick) il fiammifero; ~ n (game) la partita

meal il pasto
measure *v*(someone/something) misurare; **~ing cup** la tazza di misurazione; **~ing spoon** il misurino
mechanic il meccanico
medicine la medicina
medium (size) medio
meet *v*(someone) incontrare
meeting (corporate) la riunione; **~ room** sala riunioni
membership card la tessera associativa
memorial (place) il monumento
memory card la scheda memoria
mend *v* riparare
menstrual cramp il crampo mestruale
menu il menù
message il messaggio
meter (parking) il parchimetro
microwave il microonde
midday [BE] mezzogiorno
midnight mezzanotte
mileage il chilometraggio
mini-bar il minibar
minute il minuto
missing (was never there) mancante; scomparso **(was previously there)**
mistake l'errore
mobile mobile; **~ home** la casa prefabbricata; **~ phone [BE]** il telefonino
mobility la mobilità
money il denaro
month il mese
mop lo spazzolone
moped lo scooter

more più
morning il mattino
mosque la moschea
mother la madre
motor il motore; **~ boat** il motoscafo; **~cycle** la motocicletta; **~way [BE]** l'autostrada
mountain la montagna; **~ bike** la mountain bike
mousse (hair) la mousse
mouth la bocca
movie il film; **~ theater** il cinema
mug *v* scippare
muscle il muscolo
museum il museo
music la musica; **~ store** il negozio di musica

N

nail l'unghia; **~ file** la lima; **~ salon** il salone di bellezza
name il nome
napkin il tovagliolo
nappy [BE] il pannolino
nationality la nazionalità
nature preserve la riserva naturale
(be) nauseous *v* avere la nausea
near vicino; **~-sighted** miope
neck il collo; **~lace** la collana
need *v* necessitare
newspaper il giornale
newsstand l'edicola
next prossimo
nice sympatico
night la notte; **~club** il nightclub

no no
non-alcoholic analcolico
non-smoking non fumatori
noon mezzogiorno
north nord
nose il naso
notes [BE] le banconote
nothing niente
notify v avvertire
novice il principiante
now ora
number il numero
nurse l'infermiere

O

office l'ufficio; ~ **hours** l'orario d'ufficio
off-licence [BE] l'enoteca
oil l'olio
OK OK
old vecchio
on the corner all'angolo
once una volta
one uno; ~-**way (ticket)** solo andata; ~-**way street** il senso unico
only solo
open v aprire; ~ adj aperto
opera l'opera; ~ **house** il teatro dell'opera
opposite di fronte a
optician l'ottico
orange (color) arancione
orchestra l'orchestra
order v ordinare
outdoor pool la piscina esterna
outside fuori
over sopra; ~ **the counter**

(medication) da banco; ~**look (scenic place)** il belvedere; ~**night** per la notte
oxygen treatment l'ossigeno terapia

P

p.m. del pomeriggio
pacifier il ciuccio
pack v fare le valigie
package il pacchetto
paddling pool [BE] la piscina per bambini
pad [BE] l'assorbente
pain il dolore
pajamas il pigiama
palace il palazzo
pants i pantaloni
pantyhose il collant
paper la carta; ~ **towel** la carta da cucina
paracetamol [BE] il paracctamolo
park v parcheggiare; ~ n il parco; ~**ing garage** il parcheggio; ~**ing lot** il parcheggio
parliament building l'edificio del parlamento
part (for car) il ricambio; ~-**time** part-time
pass through v passare
passenger il passeggero
passport il passaporto; ~ **control** il controllo passaporti
password la password
pastry shop la pasticceria
path il sentiero
pay v pagare; ~ **phone** il telefono pubblico
peak (of a mountain) la vetta

pearl la perla
pedestrian il pedone
pediatrician il pediatra
pedicure il pedicure
pen la penna
penicillin la penicillina
penis il pene
per per; ~ **day** al giorno;
~ **hour** all'ora; ~ **night** a notte;
~ **week** a settimana
perfume il profumo
period (menstrual) il ciclo;
~ **(of time)** il periodo
permit v permettere
petite piccolo
petrol [BE] la benzina; ~ **station**
[BE] la stazione di servizio
pewter il peltro
pharmacy la farmacia
phone v telefonare; ~ n il
telefono; ~ **call** la telefonata;
~ **card** la scheda telefonica;
~ **number** il numero di
telefono
photo la foto; ~**copy** la fotocopia;
~**graphy** la fotografia
pick up v **(something)**
raccogliere
picnic area la zona picnic
piece il pezzo
Pill (birth control) la pillola
pillow il cuscino
**personal identification number
(PIN)** il codice PIN
pink rosa
piste [BE] la pista; ~ **map** [BE] la
cartina delle piste
pizzeria la pizzeria
place a bet v scommettere
plane l'aereo

plastic wrap la pellicola per
alimenti
plate il piatto
platform (train) il binario
platinum il platino
play v giocare; ~ n **(theater)**
lo spettacolo; ~**ground** il parco
giochi; ~**pen** il box
please per favore
pleasure il piacere
plunger lo sturalavandini
plus size la taglia forte
pocket la tasca
poison il veleno
poles (skiing) le racchette
police la polizia; ~ **report** il
verbale di polizia; ~ **station**
il commissariato
pond lo stagno
pool (swimming) la piscina
pop music la musica pop
portion la porzione
post [BE] la posta; ~ **office**
l'ufficio postale; ~**box** [BE]
la buca delle lettere; ~**card**
la cartolina
pot (for cooking) la pentola;
~ **(for flowers)** il vaso
pottery la ceramica
pounds (British sterling) le
sterline
pregnant incinta
prescribe v prescrivere
prescription la ricetta
press v **(clothing)** stirare
price il prezzo
print v stampare
problem il problema
produce la frutta e verdura;
~ **store** il fruttivendolo

prohibit v proibire
pronounce v pronunciare
public pubblico
pull v (door sign) tirare
purple viola
purse la borsetta
push v (door sign) spingere;
~**chair** [BE] il passeggino

Q

quality la qualità
question la domanda
quiet tranquillo

R

racetrack il circuito
racket (sports) la racchetta
railway station [BE] la stazione
ferroviaria
rain la pioggia; ~**coat**
l'impermeabile; ~**forest** la
foresta pluviale; ~**y** piovoso
rap (music) il rap
rape v stuprare; ~ n lo stupro
rash l'irritazione
razor blade la lametta
reach v raggiungere
ready pronto
real vero
receipt la ricevuta
receive v ricevere
reception la reception
recharge v ricaricare
recommend v raccomandare
recommendation la
raccomandazione
recycling il riciclaggio

red rosso
refrigerator il frigorifero
region la regione
registered mail la
raccomandata
regular normale
relationship la relazione
rent v affittare
rental car l'auto a noleggio
repair v riparare
repeat v ripetere
reservation la prenotazione;
~ **desk** l'ufficio prenotazioni
reserve v prenotare
restaurant il ristorante
restroom la toilette
retired in pensione
return v (something) portare
indietro; ~ n [BE] la resa
rib (body part) la costola
right (direction) a destra;
~ **of way** la precedenza
ring l'anello
river il fiume
road map la cartina stradale
rob v rubare; ~**bed** derubato
romantic romantico
room la stanza; ~ **key** la chiave
della stanza; ~ **service** il servizio
in camera
round-trip l'andata e ritorno
route il percorso
rowboat la barca a remi
rubbish [BE] la spazzatura;
~ **bag** [BE] il sacchetto per la
spazzatura
rugby il rugby
ruins le rovine
rush la fretta

S

sad triste
safe (receptacle) la cassaforte;
~ (protected) sicuro
sales tax l'IVA
same stesso
sandals i sandali
sanitary napkin l'assorbente
saucepan la pentola
sauna la sauna
save v (computer) salvare
savings (account) i risparmi
scanner lo scanner
scarf la sciarpa
schedule v programmare;
~ n il programma
school la scuola
science la scienza
scissors le forbici
sea il mare
seat il posto
security la sicurezza
see v vedere
self-service il self-service
sell v vendere
seminar il seminario
send v inviare
senior citizen l'anziano
separated (marriage) separato
serious serio
service (in a restaurant) il servizio
sexually transmitted disease
(STD) la malattia sessualmente
trasmissibile
shampoo lo shampoo
sharp appuntito
shaving cream la crema da barba
sheet (bedlinen) il lenzuolo;
~ (paper) la pagina

ship v (mail) inviare
shirt la camicia
shoes le scarpe; ~ store
il negozio di calzature
shop v fare lo shopping
shopping lo shopping; ~ area
la zona commerciale; ~ centre
[BE] il centro commerciale;
~ mall il centro commerciale
short corto; ~ sleeves le
maniche corte; ~s i pantaloncini
corti; ~-sighted [BE] miope
shoulder la spalla
show v mostrare
shower la doccia
shrine il santuario
sick malato
side il lato; ~ dish il contorno;
~ effect l'effetto collaterale;
~ order il contorno
sightseeing la visita turistica;
~ tour la gita turistica
sign v firmare
silk la seta
silver l'argento
single (marriage) single;
~ bed il letto a una piazza;
~ prints le stampe singole;
~ room la stanza singola
sink il lavandino
sister la sorella
sit v sedersi
size la taglia
skin la pelle
skirt la gonna
ski v sciare; ~ n lo sci; ~ lift lo ski lift
sleep v dormire; ~er car il vagone
letto; ~ing bag il sacco a pelo;
~ing car [BE] il vagone letto
slice (of something) la fetta
slippers le ciabatte

slow lento; **~er** più lento;
   ~ly lentamente
small piccolo; **~er** più piccolo
smoke v fumare
smoking (area) per fumatori
snack bar lo snack bar
sneakers le scarpe da ginnastica
snorkeling equipment
   l'attrezzatura da immersione
snow neve; **~board** lo
   snowboard; **~shoe** la scarpa da
   neve; **~y** nevoso
soap il sapone
soccer il calcio
sock il calzino
some qualche
soother [BE] il ciuccio
sore throat il mal di gola
sorry scusi
south sud
souvenir il souvenir; **~ store** il
   negozio di souvenir
spa la stazione termale
spatula la spatola
speak v parlare
special (food) la specialità; **~ist**
   (doctor) lo specialista
specimen il campione
speeding l'eccesso di velocità
spell v scrivere
spicy piccante
spine (body part) la spina dorsale
spoon il cucchiaio
sport lo sport; **~s massage**
   il massaggio sportivo
sporting goods store il negozio di
   articoli sportivi
sprain la storta
square quadrato; **~ kilometer**
   il chilometro quadrato; **~ meter**
   il metro quadrato

stadium lo stadio
stairs le scale
stamp v **(a ticket)** convalidare;
   ~ n **(postage)** il francobollo
start v iniziare
starter [BE] lo starter
station la stazione; **bus ~** la
   stazione dei bus; **gas ~** il benzinaio;
   petrol ~ [BE] il benzinaio; **railway**
   ~ [BE] la stazione ferroviaria;
   subway ~ la stazione della
   metropolitana **train ~** la stazione
   ferroviaria; **underground ~ [BE]** la
   stazione della metropolitana;
   ~ wagon la station wagon
statue la statua
stay v stare
steal v rubare
steep ripido
sterling silver l'argento massiccio
sting la puntura
stolen rubato
stomach lo stomaco; **~ache**
   il mal di stomaco
stop v fermarsi; **~** n la fermata
store directory la piantina del
   negozio
storey [BE] il piano
stove la cucina
straight dritto
strange strano
stream il ruscello
stroller il passeggino
student lo studente
study v studiare
stunning fenomenale
subtitle il sottotitolo
subway la metropolitana; **~ station**
   la stazione della metropolitana
suit l'abito; **~case** la valigia

sun il sole; **~block** il filtro solare; **~burn** la scottatura; **~glasses** gli occhiali da sole; **~ny** soleggiato; **~screen** il filtro solare; **~stroke** l'insolazione

super (fuel) la super; **~market** il supermercato; **~vision** la supervisione

surfboard la tavola da surf

swallow *v* ingoiare

sweater il maglione

sweatshirt la felpa

sweet (taste) dolce; **~s** [BE] le caramelle

swelling il gonfiore

swim *v* nuotare; **~suit** il costume da bagno

symbol (keyboard) il simbolo

synagogue la sinagoga

T

table il tavolo

tablet (medicine) la compressa

take *v* prendere; **~ away** [BE] portare via

tampon il tampone

taste *v* assaggiare

taxi il taxi

team la squadra

teaspoon il cucchiaino

telephone il telefono

temple (religious) il tempio

temporary provvisorio

tennis il tennis

tent la tenda; **~ peg** il picchetto da tenda; **~ pole** il paletto da tenda

terminal (airport) il terminal

terracotta la terracotta

terrible terribile

text *v* **(send a message)** inviare SMS; **~** *n* **(message)** il testo

thank *v* ringraziare; **~ you** grazie

that che

theater il teatro

theft il furto

there là

thief il ladro

thigh la coscia

thirsty assetato

this questo

throat la gola

ticket il biglietto; **~ office** la biglietteria; **~ed passenger** il passeggero con biglietto

tie (clothing) la cravatta

time il tempo; **~table** [BE] l'orario

tire lo pneumatico

tired stanco

tissue il fazzoletto di carta

tobacconist il tabaccaio

today oggi

toe il dito del piede; **~nail** l'unghia

toilet [BE] la toilette; **~ paper** la carta igienica

tomorrow domani

tongue la lingua

tonight stanotte

too troppo

tooth il dente; **~paste** il dentifricio

total (amount) il totale

tough (food) duro

tourist il turista; **~ information office** l'ufficio informazioni turistiche

tour la gita

tow truck il carro attrezzi

towel l'asciugamano

tower la torre

town la città; ~ hall il municipio;
~ map la cartina della città;
~ square la piazza della città
toy il giocattolo; ~ store il
negozio di giocattoli
track (train) il binario
traditional tradizionale
traffic light il semaforo
trail il sentiero; ~ map la mappa
dei sentieri
trailer la roulotte
train il treno; ~ station
la stazione ferroviaria
transfer v (change trains/flights)
cambiare; ~ v (money) trasferire
translate v tradurre
trash la spazzatura
travel viaggiare; ~ agency
l'agenzia viaggi; ~ sickness (air) il
mal d'aria; ~ sickness (car) il mal
d'auto; ~ sickness (sea) il mal
di mare; ~ers check il travellers
cheque
tree l'albero
trim (hair) una spuntatina
trip il viaggio
trolley [BE] il carrello
trousers i pantaloni
T-shirt la maglietta
turn off v spegnere
turn on v accendere
TV la TV
type v battere a macchina
tyre [BE] lo pneumatico

U

United Kingdom (U.K.) il Regno
Unito
United States (U.S.) gli Stati Uniti

ugly brutto
umbrella l'ombrello
unattended incustodito
unbranded medication [BE]
il farmaco generico
unconscious inconscio
underground [BE] la
metropolitana; ~ station [BE]
la stazione della metropolitana
underpants le mutande
understand v capire
underwear la biancheria intima
university l'università
unleaded (gas) senza piombo
upper superiore
upset stomach lo stomaco in
disordine
urgent urgente
use v usare
username il nome utente
utensil l'utensile

V

vacancy la disponibilità
vacation la vacanza
vaccination la vaccinazione
vacuum cleaner l'aspirapolvere
vagina la vagina
vaginal infection l'infezione vaginale
valid valido
valley la valle
valuable di valore
value il valore
VAT [BE] l'IVA
vegetarian vegetariano
vehicle registration il numero
di targa
viewpoint la prospettiva

village il villaggio
vineyard il vigneto
visa il visto
visit *v* visitare;
~**ing hours** gli orari di visita
visually impaired ipovedente
vitamin la vitamina
V-neck lo scollo a V
volleyball game la partita di pallavolo
vomit *v* vomitare

W

wait *v* attendere; ~ *n* l'attesa;
~**ing room** la sala d'attesa
waiter il cameriere
waitress la cameriera
wake *v* svegliare, svegliarsi;
~**-up call** il servizio sveglia
walk *v* camminare; ~ *n* la passeggiata; ~**ing route** il percorso pedonale
wall clock l'orologio da parete
wallet il portafogli
warm *v* (something) riscaldare;
~ *adj* (temperature) caldo
washing machine la lavatrice
watch l'orologio
water skis lo sci d'acqua
waterfall la cascata
weather il tempo
week la settimana; ~**end** il fine settimana; ~**ly** settimanalmente
welcome *v* accogliere
well-rested ben riposato
west ovest
what (question) cosa

wheelchair la sedia a rotelle; ~ **ramp** la rampa per sedia a rotelle
when (question) quando
where (question) dove
white bianco; ~ **gold** l'oro bianco
who (question) chi
widowed vedovo
wife la moglie
window la finestra; ~ **case** la vetrina
windsurfer il windsurf
wine list la carta dei vini
wireless wireless; ~ **internet** l'Internet wireless; ~ **internet service** il servizio Internet wireless; ~ **phone** il telefono cordless
with con
withdraw *v* ritirare; ~**al (bank)** il prelievo
without senza
woman la donna
wool la lana
work *v* lavorare
wrap *v* incartare
wrist il polso
write *v* scrivere

Y

year l'anno
yellow giallo; ~ **gold** l'oro giallo
yes sì
yesterday ieri
young giovane
youth hostel l'ostello della gioventù

Z

zoo lo zoo

Italian–English Dictionary

A

a buon mercato inexpensive
a destra right (direction)
a girocollo crew neck
a notte per night
a settimana per week
a sinistra left (direction)
a tempo pieno full-time
l'abbazia abbey
l'abbigliamento clothing
abbracciare to hug
l'abito suit
accendere v light (cigarette);
  ~ v turn on (lights)
l'accendino lighter
accessibile ai disabili
  handicapped- [disabled BE]
  accessible
l'accesso access
accettare v accept
accogliere v welcome
l'acconciatura hairstyle
l'acconto cash advance
l'acqua water; ~ calda hot
  water; ~ potabile drinking water;
  ~scooter jet ski
l'adattatore adapter
addebitare v charge (credit card)
l'aereo airplane
l'aeroporto airport
affamato hungry
affittare v rent [hire BE]
l'agenzia agency; ~ viaggi
  travel agency
l'aggressione attack (on person)

l'agopuntura acupuncture
l'AIDS AIDS
aiutare to help
l'aiuto n help
al giorno per day
l'albero tree
all'angolo on the corner
allattare breastfeed
allergico allergic
l'alloggio accommodation
all'ora per hour
alto high
amare v love (someone)
l'ambulanza ambulance
americano American
l'amico friend
l'amore n love
analcolico non-alcoholic
andare v go (somewhere);
  ~ bene fit (clothing)
l'andata e ritorno round-trip
l'anello ring
anemico anemic
l'anestesia anesthesia
l'animale animal
l'anno year
annullare v cancel
l'antibiotico antibiotic
l'antipasto appetizer [starter BE]
l'anziano senior citizen
aperto adj open
l'appartamento apartment
l'appendice appendix (body part)
l'appuntamento appointment
appuntito sharp
l'apribottiglie bottle opener
aprire v open
l'apriscatole can opener
arancione orange (color)

l'argento silver; **~ massiccio** sterling silver

l'aria condizionata air conditioning

l'armadietto locker; **~ dei bagagli** luggage locker

l'aromaterapia aromatherapy

arrivare *v* arrive

arrivederla goodbye

gli arrivi arrivals (airport)

l'arte art

l'arteria artery

gli articoli casalinghi household goods

l'artrite arthritis

l'ascensore elevator

l'asciugacapelli hair dryer

l'asciugamano towel

asmatico asthmatic

l'aspirapolvere vacuum cleaner

l'aspirina aspirin

assaggiare *v* taste

l'assegno *n* check (payment) [cheque BE]

assetato thirsty

l'assicurazione insurance

l'assorbente sanitary napkin [pad BE]

l'astuccio della macchina fotografica camera case

attendere *v* wait

l'attesa *n* wait

attraente attractive

l'attrattiva attraction (place); **~ principale** main attraction

l'attrezzatura equipment; **~ da immersione** snorkeling equipment; **~ subacquea** diving equipment

gli auricolari headphones

Australia Australia

australiano Australian

l'auto car; **~bus** bus; **~ con il cambio automatico** automatic car; **~ con il cambio manuale** manual car; **~ a noleggio** rental [hire BE] car

automatico automatic

l'autonoleggio car rental [hire BE]

l'autostrada highway [motorway BE]

avere *v* have; **~ la nausea** *v* be nauseous

avvertire *v* notify

l'avvocato lawyer

B

la babysitter babysitter

baciare *v* kiss

il bagaglio luggage [baggage BE]; **~ a mano** carry-on [hand luggage BE]

il bagnino lifeguard

il bagno bathroom

ballare *v* dance

il ballo dancing

il balsamo conditioner

il bambino child

la bambola doll

la banca bank

il bancomat ATM, ATM card, debit card

la banconota *n* bill (money) [note BE]

il bar bar; **~ per gay** gay bar

il barbecue barbecue

il barbiere barber

la barca boat; **~ a remi** rowboat

il baseball baseball

il basketball basketball

basso low
i bastoncini cinesi chopsticks
battere a macchina *v* type
la batteria battery
il bebè baby
beige beige
bello beautiful
il belvedere overlook
  (scenic place)
ben riposato well-rested
la benda bandage
bene good
la benzina gas (vehicle)
  [petrol BE]
il benzinaio gas [petrol BE]
  station
bere *v* drink
la bevanda *n* drink
la biancheria intima
  underwear
bianco white
il biberon baby bottle
la biblioteca library
il bicchiere glass (drinking)
la bicicletta bicycle
la biglietteria ticket office
il biglietto ticket; ~ **del bus** bus
  ticket; ~ **elettronico** e-ticket;
  ~ **da visita** business card
il bikini bikini
il binario platform; track (train)
blu blue
la bocca mouth
la borsa bag
la borsetta purse [handbag BE]
il bosco forest
la bottiglia bottle
il box playpen
il braccialetto bracelet

il braccio arm
bruciare *v* burn
brutto ugly
la buca delle lettere postbox
buongiorno good morning
buon pomeriggio good afternoon
buonasera good evening
buono *adj* good
il bus espresso express bus
la busta envelope

C

il cabaret cabaret
la cabina cabin
il caffè cafe, coffee
il calcio soccer
caldo hot (temperature)
il calore heat [heating BE]
le calorie calories
il calzino sock
cambiare *v* change;
  ~ *v* exchange; ~ *v* transfer
il cambio *n* change (money);
  ~ *n* exchange (place);
  ~ **valuta** currency exchange
la cameriera waitress
il cameriere waiter
la camicetta blouse
la camicia shirt
camminare *v* walk
campeggiare *v* camp
il campeggio campsite
il campione specimen
il campo field (sports);
  ~ **da golf** golf course;
  ~ **di battaglia** battleground
il Canada Canada

canadese Canadian
il **canalone** canyon
cancellare v clear (on an ATM)
il **cane da guida** guide dog
i **capelli** hair
capire v understand
il **cappello** hat
il **cappotto** coat
la **caraffa** carafe
le **caramelle** candy [sweet BE]
il **carbone** charcoal
carino cute
caro expensive
il **carrello** cart [trolley BE];
  ~ **bagagli** luggage cart
il **carro attrezzi** tow truck
la **carta** card, paper; ~ **di**
  credito credit card; ~ **da**
  cucina paper towel;
  ~ **igienica** toilet paper;
  ~ **d'imbarco** boarding pass;
  ~ **stagnola** aluminum [kitchen
  BE] foil; ~ **dei vini** wine list
la **cartina** map; ~ **della**
  città town map; ~ **delle**
  piste trail [piste BE] map;
  ~ **stradale** road map
la **cartolina** postcard
il **cartone** carton
la **casa** house
la **cascata** waterfall
il **casco** helmet
il **casinò** casino
la **cassa** case (container);
  ~**forte** safe (for valuables)
la **cassetta della posta** mailbox
il **cassiere** cashier
il **castello** castle
la **cattedrale** cathedral
il **cavatappi** corkscrew

la **caviglia** ankle
il **CD** CD
Celsius Celsius
la **cena** dinner
il **centimetro** centimeter
il **centro** downtown area;
  ~ **business** business center;
  ~ **commerciale** shopping mall
  [centre BE]
la **ceramica** pottery
la **ceretta** wax; ~ **all'inguine**
  bikini wax; ~ **per sopracciglie**
  eyebrow wax
il **certificato** certificate
il **cestino** basket (grocery store)
che that
il **check-in** check-in (hotel/airport)
chi who
chiamare v call
la **chiamata** n call
la **chiave** key; ~ **elettronica** key
  card; ~ **della stanza** room key
la **chiesa** church
il **chilo** kilo; ~**grammo** kilogram;
  ~**metraggio** mileage;
  ~**metro** kilometer; ~**metro**
  quadrato square kilometer
chiudere v close (a shop); ~ v lock
chiuso closed
le **ciabatte** slippers
ciao hi, bye
il **cibo** food
il **ciclismo** cycling
il **ciclo** period (menstrual)
il **cinema** movie theater
cinese Chinese
la **cintura** belt
il **circuito** racetrack
la **città** town
il **ciuccio** pacifier [soother BE]

la classe class; ~ business business class; ~ economica economy class

il club club; ~ di ballo dance club; ~ jazz jazz club; ~ per gay gay club

il codice code; ~ di abbigliamento dress code; ~ PIN personal identification number (PIN)

la coincidenza connection (flight)

la colazione breakfast

la collana necklace

il collant pantyhose

il collega colleague

il collegamento connection (internet); ~ wireless a Internet wireless internet

collegarsi v connect (internet)

la collina hill

il collo neck

la colonia cologne

il colore color

il coltello knife

come how

il commissariato police station

la compagnia aerea airline

la compagnia di assicurazione insurance company

compilare v fill out (form)

il compleanno birthday

comporre il numero v dial

comprare v buy

la compressa tablet (medicine)

il computer computer

con with

il concerto concert

la condizione condition (medical)

la conferenza conference

confermare v confirm

la congestione congestion

il consolato consulate

il consulente consultant

contagioso contagious

i contanti n cash

contattare to contact

il conto n bill (of sale); ~ account; ~ corrente checking [current BE] account

il contorno side dish

controllare v check (luggage)

il controllo passaporti passport control

convalidare v stamp (a ticket)

la coperta blanket

il coperto cover charge

la coppa bowl

il corridoio aisle

corto short

cosa what (question)

la coscia thigh

costare v cost

costipato constipated

il costo charge (cost)

la costola rib (body part)

il costume da bagno swimsuit

il cotone cotton

il crampo mestruale menstrual cramp

la cravatta tie (clothing)

la crema cream (ointment); ~ antisettica antiseptic cream; ~ da barba shaving cream

il cristallo crystal

la cuccetta berth

il cucchiaino teaspoon

il cucchiaio spoon

la cucina kitchen, stove

cucinare v cook

la culla crib

la c
il dis
[dis

il cuore heart
il cuscino pillow

D

da banco over the counter
  (medication)
danneggiare v damage
danneggiato damaged
dare v give; ~ da mangiare
  v feed
la data date (calendar)
del pomeriggio p.m.
il denaro money
il dente tooth
la dentiera denture
il dentifricio toothpaste
il dentista dentist
il deodorante deodorant
depositare v deposit
il deposito n deposit
derubato robbed
il deserto desert
il detersivo detergent;
  ~ per i piatti dishwashing liquid
di fronte a opposite
di valore valuable
diabetico diabetic
il diamante diamond
la diarrea diarrhea
dichiarare v declare
il diesel diesel
dietro around (the corner), behind
  (direction)
difficile difficult
digitale digital
direzione direction
ile handicapped
BE]

la disponibilità vacancy
il disturbo cardiaco heart
  condition
il dito finger; ~ del piede toe
divorziare v divorce
la doccia shower
la dogana customs
dolce sweet (taste)
il dollaro dollar (U.S.)
il dolore hurt (pain);
  ~ al petto chest pain
la domanda question
domani tomorrow
domestico domestic
la donna woman
dopo after; ~barba aftershave
doppiato dubbed
dormire v sleep
il dormitorio dormitory
dove where (question)
la dozzina dozen
dritto straight
durante during
duro tough (food)
duty-free duty-free
il DVD DVD

E

l'eccesso excess; ~ di velocità
  speeding
economico cheap
l'edicola newsstand
l'edificio building; ~ del
  parlamento parliament building
l'effetto collaterale side effect
eliminare v delete (computer)
l'e-mail n e-mail
l'emergenza emergency

l'enoteca liquor store
[off-licence BE]
entrare *v* enter
l'entrata entrance
l'erboristeria health food store
l'errore mistake
esausto exhausted
l'escursione excursion;
~ in pullman bus tour
esperto expert
espresso express
essere *v* be
est east
estrarre *v* extract (tooth)
l'età age
l'euro euro
extra extra; ~ large extra large

F

facile easy
la famiglia family
fare *v* do; ~ l'autostop
v hitchhike; ~ la ceretta *v* wax;
~ un incidente *v* crash (car);
~ il logoff *v* log off (computer);
~ il logon *v* log on (computer);
~ lo shopping *v* shop;
~ le valigie *v* pack
la farmacia pharmacy
[chemist BE]
il fast food fast food
la fattoria farm
la fattura bill [invoice BE]
fatturare *v* bill (charge)
il fax *n* fax
il fazzoletto di carta tissue
la febbre fever
il fegato liver (body part)

felice happy
la felpa sweatshirt
fenomenale stunning
fermarsi *v* stop
la fermata *n* stop; ~ del bus bus
stop
il ferro da stiro *n* iron (clothes)
la fetta slice (of something)
il fiammifero *n* match (wooden
stick)
il film movie
il filtro solare sunblock,
sunscreen
il fine settimana weekend
la finestra window
finire *v* end
il fiore flower
firmare *v* sign
il fiume river
la fontana fountain
le forbici scissors
la forchetta fork
la foresta pluviale rainforest
il fornello da
campeggio camping stove
la fortezza fort
la foto photo; ~ digitale digital
photo; ~copia photocopy;
~grafia photography
il francobollo *n* stamp (postage)
il fratello brother
freddo cold (temperature)
il freezer freezer
i freni brakes (car)
frequentare to attend
fresco cool (temperature);
~ fresh
la fretta rush
il frigorifero refrigerator

la frutta e verdura produce
il fruttivendolo grocery store
fumare *v* smoke
la funivia cable car
il fuoco fire
fuori outside
il furto theft; ~ con scasso
   break-in (burglary)

G

la gamba leg
la gara di golf golf tournament
il garage garage
il gas gas (heating);
   ~ per cucina cooking gas
la gastronomia delicatessen
gay gay
il gel gel (hair)
gelato icy
il ghiaccio ice
la giacca jacket
giallo yellow
il giardino botanico botanical
   garden
il ginecologo gynecologist
il ginocchio knee
giocare *v* play
il giocattolo toy
la gioielleria jewelry
il gioielliere jeweler
il giornale newspaper
il giorno day
giovane young
la gita tour; ~ turistica
   sightseeing tour
il giubbotto di salvataggio life
   jacket
la giuntura joint (body part)

la goccia drop (medicine)
godersi *v* enjoy
la gola throat
il gomito elbow
la gomma rubber; ~ a terra flat
   tire; ~ da masticare chewing gum
il gonfiore swelling
la gonna skirt
i gradi degrees (temperature)
il grammo gram
grande big, large;
   ~ magazzino department store
grazie thank you
grigio gray
la grotta cave
il gruppo group
guardare *v* look
il guasto breakdown
la guida guide, guide book
guidare *v* drive

H

l'hockey hockey;
   ~ su ghiaccio ice hockey
l'hotel hotel

I

l'ibuprofene ibuprofen
l'identificazione identification
ieri yesterday
imbarcarsi *v* board
l'impermeabile raincoat
in in; ~ pensione retired
incartare *v* wrap
incassare *v* cash
l'incidente accident

incidere v engrave
incinta pregnant
includere v include
inconscio unconscious
incontrare v meet (someone)
l'incontro di boxe boxing match
l'incrocio intersection
incustodito unattended
l'indirizzo address;
~ **e-mail** e-mail address
infastidire v bother
l'infermiere nurse
infetto infected
l'infezione vaginale vaginal infection
le informazioni information (phone)
inglese British, English
ingoiare v swallow
l'ingresso admission
iniziare v begin, start
inserire v insert
l'insetto bug
insipido bland
l'insolazione sunstroke
l'insonnia insomnia
l'insulina insulin
interessante interesting
intermedio intermediate
internazionale international (airport area)
l'Internet internet; ~ **caffè** internet cafe; ~ **wireless** wireless internet
l'interno extension (phone)
l'interprete interpreter
l'intestino intestine
intollerante al lattosio lactose intolerant

l'intrattenimento entertainment
inviare v send, ship (mail);
~ **e-mail** v e-mail; ~ **per fax** v fax; ~ **SMS** v text (send a message)
ipermetrope far- [long- BE] sighted
ipovedente visually impaired
l'ippodromo horsetrack
l'Irlanda Ireland
irlandese Irish
l'irritazione rash
l'Italia Italy
italiano Italian
l'IVA sales tax [VAT BE]

J

il jazz jazz
i jeans jeans

L

là there
la casa prefabbricata mobile home
la stanza singola single room
il labbro lip
la lacca hairspray
il ladro thief
il lago lake
la lametta razor blade; ~ **usa e getta** disposable razor
la lampadina lightbulb
la lana wool
il latte in polvere formula (baby)
il lato side
la lavanderia laundry;
~ **a gettone** laundromat [launderette BE]

il lavandino sink
il lavasecco dry cleaner
la lavastoviglie dishwasher
la lavatrice washing machine
lavorare *v* work
il lavoro business
lentamente slowly
la lente lens; **~ a contatto** contact lens
il lenzuolo sheet
la lettera letter
il lettino cot
il letto bed; **~ matrimoniale** double bed; **~ a una piazza** single bed
la lezione lesson
libero available, free
la libreria bookstore
il libro book
il lift pass lift pass
la lima nail file
la linea line (train)
la lingua tongue
il lino linen
il litro liter
locale local
lontano far
la lozione lotion
la luce light (overhead)
il lunapark amusement park
lungo long

M

la macchina fotografica camera; **~ digitale** digital camera
il macellaio butcher
la madre mother
la maglietta T-shirt

il maglione sweater
magnifico magnificent
il mal sickness; **~ d'aria** motion sickness (air); **~ d'auto** motion sickness (car); **~ di gola** sore throat; **~ di mare** motion sickness (sea);
~ d'orecchio earache;
~ di schiena backache;
~ di stomaco stomachache;
~ di testa headache
malato sick [ill BE]
malattia sessualmente trasmissibile sexually transmitted disease (STD)
mancante missing
mangiare *v* eat
le maniche sleeves; **~ corte** short sleeves; **~ lunghe** long sleeves
il manicure manicure
la mano hand
il mare sea
il marito husband
marrone brown
il martello hammer
la mascella jaw
il massaggio massage;
~ sportivo sports massage
il mattino morning
del mattino a.m.
il meccanico mechanic
la medicina medicine
il medico doctor
medio medium (size)
meno less
il menù menu; **~ delle bevande** drink menu; **~ per bambini** children's menu
il mercato market

le merci goods
il mese month
la messa mass (church service)
il messaggio message;
~ istantaneo instant message
la metà half
il metro quadrato square meter
la metropolitana subway
[underground BE]
la mezz'ora half hour
la mezzanotte midnight
il mezzo chilo half-kilo
mezzogiorno noon [midday BE]
il microonde microwave
migliore better
il migliore best
il minibar mini-bar
Il mlnuto minute
miope near- [short- BE] sighted
misurare v measure (someone,
something)
il misurino measuring spoon
mobile mobile
la mobilità mobility
i mocassini loafers
il mocio mop
modificare v alter (clothing)
il modulo form (fill-in)
la moglie wife
la moneta coin
la montagna mountain
il monumento memorial (place)
la moschea mosque
mostrare v show
la motocicletta motorcycle
il motore motor
il motoscafo motor boat
la mountain bike mountain
bike

la mousse mousse (hair)
la multa fine (fee for breaking
law)
il municipio town hall
il muscolo muscle
il museo museum
la musica music; ~ classica
classical music; ~ folk folk
music; ~ pop pop music
le mutande underpants

N

il naso nose
il nastro trasportatore
conveyor belt
le natiche buttocks
la nazionalità nationality
necessitare v need
il negozio store; ~ d'abbigliamento
clothing store; ~ d'antiquariato
antique store; ~ di articoli da
regalo gift shop; ~ di articoli
sportivi sporting goods store;
~ di calzature shoe store;
~ di fotografia camera store;
~ di giocattoli toy store;
~ di musica music store;
~ di souvenir souvenir store
nero black
la neve snow
nevoso snowy
niente nothing
il nightclub nightclub
il nipote grandchild
no no
noioso boring
il nome name;
~ utente username
non fumatori non-smoking

il **nonno** grandparent
nord north
normale regular
la **notte** night
il **numero** number; ~ **di fax** fax
   number; ~ **di patente** driver's
   license number; ~ **di targa**
   vehicle registration; ~ **di**
   telefono phone number
nuotare v swim

O

gli **occhiali** glasses;
   ~ **da sole** sunglasses
l'**occhio** eye
oggi today
OK OK
l'**olio** oil
l'**ombrello** umbrella
l'**opera** opera
ora now
l'**ora** hour
gli **orari di visita** visiting hours
l'**orario** schedule [timetable BE];
   ~ **d'apertura** business hours;
   ~ **d'ufficio** office hours
l'**orchestra** orchestra
ordinare v order
gli **orecchini** earrings
l'**orecchio** ear
l'**oro** gold; ~**bianco** white gold;
   ~ **giallo** yellow gold
l'**orologio** watch;
   ~ **da parete** wall clock
l'**ospedale** hospital
l'**osso** bone
l'**ostello** hostel; ~ **della gioventù**
   youth hostel
l'**ottico** optician

l'**otturazione** filling (tooth)
ovest west

P

il **pacchetto** package
la **padella** frying pan
il **padre** father
il **pagamento del conto** check-
   out (hotel)
pagare v pay
il **palazzo** palace
la **palestra** gym
il **paletto da tenda** tent pole
la **panetteria** bakery
il **pannolino** diaper [nappy BE]
i **pantaloncini corti** shorts
i **pantaloni** pants [trousers BE]
il **paracetamolo** acetaminophen
   [paracetamol BE]
parcheggiare v park
il **parcheggio** parking garage;
   ~ parking lot [car park BE]
il **parco** n park; ~ **giochi**
   playground
parlare v speak
il **parrucchiere** hair salon
le **partenze** departures (airport)
partire v leave
la **partita** game, match; ~ **di**
   football soccer [football game BE];
   ~ **di pallavolo** volleyball game
part-time part-time
il **passaggio** lift
il **passaporto** passport
passare v pass through
il **passeggero** passenger; ~ **con**
   biglietto ticketed passenger
la **passeggiata** n walk

il passeggino stroller [pushchair BE]

la password password

la pasticceria pastry shop

il pasto meal

il pediatra pediatrician

il pedicure pedicure

il pedone pedestrian

la pelle leather, skin

la pellicola per alimenti plastic wrap [cling film BE]

il peltro pewter

il pene penis

la penicillina penicillin

la penna pen

la pensione bed and breakfast

la pentola saucepan, pot

per for, per; **~ favore** please; **~ fumatori** smoking (area); **~ la notte** overnight

il percorso route; **~ alternativo** alternate route; **~ ciclabile** bike route; **~ pedonale** walking route

perdere v lose (something)

la perdita discharge (bodily fluid)

pericoloso dangerous

il periodo period (of time)

la perla pearl

permettere v allow, permit

perso lost

il pettine comb

il petto chest (body part)

il petto breast

il pezzo piece

piacere v like

il piacere pleasure

il piano floor [storey BE]

il pianterreno ground floor

la piantina del negozio store directory

il piatto plate; **~ principale** main course

la piazza della città town square

piccante hot (spicy)

il picchetto da tenda tent peg

piccolo little, petite, small

il piede foot

il pigiama pajamas

la pillola Pill (birth control)

la pioggia rain

piovoso rainy

la piscina pool; **~ per bambini** kiddie [paddling BE] pool; **~ esterna** outdoor pool; **~ interna** indoor pool

pista piste [BE]

più more; **~ basso** lower; **~ economico** cheaper; **~ forte** louder; **~ grande** bigger; **~ lento** slower; **~ piccolo** smaller; **~ tardi** later; **~ veloce** faster

la pizzeria pizzeria

il pizzo lace

il platino platinum

lo pneumatico tire [tyre BE]

la polizia police

il polmone lung

il polso wrist

il pomeriggio afternoon

la pompa dell'aria air pump

il ponte bridge

la porta door; **~ antincendio** fire door

il portachiavi key ring

il portafogli wallet

portare v bring; **~ indietro** v return (something); **~ via** to go [take away BE]

la porzione portion; **~ per bambini** children's portion
la posa exposure (film)
la posta *n* mail [post BE]; **~ aerea** airmail
il posto seat; **~ sul corridoio** aisle seat
il pranzo lunch
la precedenza right of way
il prefisso area code; **~ del paese** country code
il prelievo withdrawal (bank)
prendere *v* take
prenotare *v* reserve
la prenotazione reservation
la presa elettrica electric outlet
prescrivere *v* prescribe
presentare *v* introduce
il preservativo condom
la pressione sanguigna blood pressure
presto early
la previsione forecast
il prezzo price
prima before, earlier; **~ classe** first class
primo first
il principiante beginner, novice
il problema problem
i prodotti per la pulizia cleaning supplies
profondamente deeply
il profumo perfume
il programma *n* schedule
programmare *v* schedule
proibire *v* prohibit
pronto ready
pronunciare *v* pronounce
la prospettiva viewpoint
prossimo next

provvisorio temporary
pubblico public
pulire *v* clean
pulito *adj* clean
la pulizia del viso facial
la puntura sting; **~ d'insetto** insect bite

Q

quadrato square
qualche some
la qualità quality
qualsiasi cosa anything
quando when (question)
quanto how much (question)
questo this
qui here

R

la racchetta racket (sports)
le racchette poles (skiing)
raccogliere *v* pick up (something)
raccomandare *v* recommend
la raccomandata registered mail
la raccomandazione recommendation
il radiatore heater
il raffreddore cold (sickness)
la ragazza girl, girlfriend
il ragazzo boy, boyfriend
raggiungere *v* reach (get hold of)
il rame copper
la rampa per sedia a rotelle wheelchair ramp
il rap rap (music)

la reazione allergica allergic reaction
la reception reception
il reclamo complaint
il regalo gift
il reggiseno bra
la regione region
il Regno Unito United Kingdom (U.K.)
la relazione relationship
il rene kidney (body part)
il repellente per gli insetti insect repellent
il residente UE EU resident
respirare *v* breathe
il ricambio part (for car)
il riciclaggio *n* recycling
la ricetta prescription
ricevere *v* receive
la ricevuta receipt
il riciclaggio *n* recycling
riempire *v* fill
rifiutare *v* decline (credit card)
ringraziare *v* thank
riparare *v* fix, mend, repair
ripetere *v* repeat
ripido steep
il responsabile manager
il riscaldamento heating
riscaldare *v* warm (something)
la riserva naturale nature preserve
i risparmi savings (account)
il ristorante restaurant
ritardare *v* delay
ritirare *v* withdraw
il ritiro bagagli baggage claim
la riunione meeting
la rivista magazine

romantico romantic
rompere *v* break
rosa pink
rosso red
rotto broken
la roulotte trailer
le rovine ruins
rubare *v* rob, steal
rubato stolen
il rugby rugby
il rullino film (camera)
il ruscello stream

S

il sacchetto per i rifiuti garbage [rubbish BE] bag
il sacco a pelo sleeping bag
la sala room; **~ congressi** convention hall; **~ d'attesa** waiting room; **~ da concerti** concert hall; **~ da pranzo** dining room; **~ giochi** arcade; **~ riunioni** meeting room
il salone di bellezza nail salon
la salute health
Salute! Cheers!
salvare *v* save (computer)
salve hello
la salvietta per neonati baby wipe
i sandali sandals
il sangue blood
sanguinare *v* bleed
il santuario shrine
il sapone soap
la sauna sauna
la sbornia hangover
le scale stairs; **~ mobili** escalators

lo **scanner** scanner
le **scarpe** shoes;
  ~ **da neve** snowshoes;
  ~ **basse** flat shoes; ~ **col tacco
  alto** high-heeled shoes;
  ~ **da ginnastica** sneakers
gli **scarponi da montagna** hiking
  boots
la **scatola** box
lo **scatolame** canned good
scendere v get off (a train, bus,
  subway)
la **scheda** card; ~ **memoria**
  memory card; ~ **telefonica**
  phone card
lo **schermo** display
la **schiena** back (body part)
lo **sci** n ski; ~ **d'acqua** water skis
sciare v ski
la **sciarpa** scarf
la **scienza** science
scippare v mug
la **scogliera** cliff
la **scolapasta** colander
scollegare v disconnect
  (computer)
lo **scollo a V** V-neck
scommettere v place a bet
scomparso missing
lo **sconto** discount
lo **scontrino bagagli** luggage
  [baggage BE] ticket
lo **scooter** moped
la **scopa** broom
la **scottatura** sunburn
scrivere v spell, write
la **scuola** school
scuro dark
scusare v excuse
scusi sorry (apology)

sedersi v sit
la **sedia** chair; ~ **a
  rotelle** wheelchair;
  ~ **a sdraio** deck chair
il **sedile per bambino** child's
  seat
il **seggiolino per auto** car seat
il **seggiolone** highchair
la **seggiovia** chair lift
il **self-service** self-service
il **semaforo** traffic light
il **seminario** seminar
il **senso unico** one-way street
il **sentiero** path, trail
senza without; ~ **grassi** fat free;
  ~ **piombo** unleaded (gas)
separato separated (marriage)
la **sera** evening
serio serious
la **serratura** n lock
i **servizi di pulizia
  domestica** housekeeping
  services
il **servizio** service (in a restaurant);
  ~ **completo** full-service;
  ~ **di lavanderia** laundry service;
  ~ **in camera** room service;
  ~ **Internet** internet service;
  ~ **Internet wireless** wireless
  internet service; ~ **sveglia**
  wake-up call
la **seta** silk
la **settimana** week
settimanalmente weekly
lo **shampoo** shampoo
lo **shopping** shopping
sì yes
la **sicurezza** security
sicuro safe (protected)
la **sigaretta** cigarette

il sigaro cigar
il simbolo symbol (keyboard)
la sinagoga synagogue
single single (marriage)
lo ski lift drag lift, ski lift
lo slip briefs (clothing)
lo smalto enamel (jewelry)
lo snack bar snack bar
lo snowboard snowboard
il sole sun
soleggiato sunny
solo alone, only; ~ andata one-way (ticket)
la soluzione per lenti a contatto contact lens solution
la sonnolenza drowsiness
sopra over
sordo deaf
la sorella sister
il sottotitolo subtitle
il souvenir souvenir
la spalla shoulder
la spatola spatula
la spazzatura trash [rubbish BE]
la spazzola hairbrush
lo specialista specialist (doctor)
la specialità special (food)
spedire v mail
spegnere v turn off (lights)
lo spettacolo n play (theater); ~ di danza ballet
la spiaggia beach
la spilla brooch
la spina dorsale spine (body part)
spingere v push (door sign)
lo spogliatoio fitting room
sporco dirty
lo sport sport

sposare v marry
sposato married
la spuntatina trim (hair)
la squadra team
squisito delicious
lo stadio stadium
lo stagno pond
stampare v print
la stampa n print; ~ digitale digital print; ~ singola single print
stanco tired
stanotte tonight
la stanza room
stare v stay
gli Stati Uniti United States (U.S.)
la station wagon station wagon [estate car BE]
la statua statue
la stazione station; ~ degli autobus bus station; ~ dei bus bus station; ~ ferroviaria train station [railway station BE]; ~ della metropolitana subway station [underground station BE]; ~ di servizio gas station [petrol station BE]; ~ termale spa
la stecca di sigarette carton of cigarettes
le sterline pounds (British sterling)
stesso same
stirare v iron, press (clothing)
gli stivali boots
lo stomaco stomach; ~ in disordine upset stomach
stordito dizzy
la storta sprain
strano strange
straordinario amazing
lo studente student

studiare *v* study
stuprare *v* rape
lo stupro *n* rape
lo sturalavandini plunger
sud south
la super super (fuel)
superiore upper
il supermercato supermarket
la supervisione supervision
svegliare, svegliarsi *v* wake
sviluppare *v* develop (film)
svuotare *v* empty

T

il tabaccaio tobacconist
la taglia size; **~ forte** plus size
tagliare *v* cut (hair)
il taglio *n* cut (injury), haircut
il tampone tampon
tardi late (time)
la tariffa fee
la tasca pocket
la tassa duty (tax)
il tasso di cambio exchange rate
la tavola da surf surfboard
il tavolo table
il taxi taxi
la tazza cup; **~ di misurazione** measuring cup
il teatro theater; **~ dell'opera** opera house
telefonare *v* phone
la telefonata phone call
il telefonino cell [mobile BE] phone

il telefono *n* phone;
~ telephone; **~ cordless** wireless phone;
~ pubblico pay phone
il telone impermeabile groundcloth [groundsheet BE]
il tempio temple (religious)
il tempo time, weather
la tenda tent
il tennis tennis
la terapia ad ossigeno oxygen treatment
le terme hot spring
il terminal terminal (airport)
la terracotta terracotta
terribile terrible
la tessera card; **~ associativa** membership card;
~ dell'assicurazione insurance card; **~ internazionale dello studente** international student card
la testa head (body part)
il testo *n* text (message)
tirare *v* pull (door sign)
la toilette restroom [toilet BE]
la torcia elettrica flashlight
la torre tower
la tosse *n* cough
tossire *v* cough
il totale total (amount)
il tovagliolo napkin
tradizionale traditional
tradurre *v* translate
il traghetto ferry
tranquillo quiet
trasferire *v* transfer (money)

il travellers cheque travelers check [travelers cheque BE]
il treno train; **~ espresso** express train
triste sad
troppo too
tuffarsi v dive
il turista tourist
la TV TV

U

l'uccello bird
l'ufficio office; **~ di cambio** currency exchange office; **~ informazioni** information desk; **~ informazioni turistiche** tourist information office; **~ oggetti smarriti** lost and found; **~ postale** post office; **~ prenotazioni** reservation desk
ultimo last
una volta once
l'unghia fingernail, toenail
unire v join
l'università university
uno one
l'uomo man
urgente urgent
usa e getta disposable
usare v use
uscire v exit
l'uscita gate (airport), exit; **~ d'emergenza** emergency exit
l'utensile utensil

V

la vacanza vacation [holiday BE]
la vaccinazione vaccination
la vagina vagina
il vagone letto sleeper [sleeping BE] car
valido valid
la valigia suitcase
la valle valley
il valore value
la valuta currency
il vaso jar
vecchio old
vedere v see
vedovo widowed
vegetariano vegetarian
il veleno poison
veloce fast
vendere v sell
venire v come
il ventaglio fan (souvenir)
il ventilatore fan (appliance)
il verbale di polizia police report
verde green
vero real
la vescica bladder
il vestito dress (piece of clothing)
la vetrina window case
la vetrinetta display case
il vetro glass (material)
la vetta peak (of a mountain)
il viaggio trip
vicino close, near, nearby, next to
i vigili del fuoco fire department
il vigneto vineyard

il **villaggio** village
viola purple
la **visita turistica** sightseeing
visitare *v* visit
il **viso** face
il **visto** visa
la **vita** life
la **vitamina** vitamin
vivere *v* live
il **volo** flight; ~ **internazionale** international flight; ~ **nazionale** domestic flight
vomitare *v* vomit

W

il **WC da campeggio** chemical toilet
il **windsurf** windsurfer

Z

lo **zaino** backpack
la **zona** area; ~ **commerciale** shopping area; ~ **picnic** picnic area
lo **zoo** zoo